T0193984

Wasted Years

My Journey to Heaven

Duane Clarke

WESTBOW
PRESS®
A DIVISION OF THOMAS NELSON
& ZONDERVAN

This book is a work of non-fiction. Unless otherwise noted, the author
and the publisher make no explicit guarantees as to the accuracy of
the information contained in this book and in some cases, names of
people and places have been altered to protect their privacy.

THE HOLY BIBLE, NEW INTERNATIONAL VERSION®,
NIV® Copyright © 1973, 1978, 1984, 2011 by Biblica, Inc.®
Used by permission. All rights reserved worldwide.

Scripture taken from the King James Version of the Bible.

WestBow Press books may be ordered through booksellers or by contacting:

WestBow Press
A Division of Thomas Nelson & Zondervan
1663 Liberty Drive
Bloomington, IN 47403
www.westbowpress.com
1 (866) 928-1240

Because of the dynamic nature of the Internet, any web addresses or
links contained in this book may have changed since publication and
may no longer be valid. The views expressed in this work are solely those
of the author and do not necessarily reflect the views of the publisher,
and the publisher hereby disclaims any responsibility for them.

Any people depicted in stock imagery provided by Getty Images are
models, and such images are being used for illustrative purposes only.
Certain stock imagery © Getty Images.

ISBN: 978-1-9736-2051-8 (sc)
ISBN: 978-1-9736-2052-5 (hc)
ISBN: 978-1-9736-2053-2 (e)

Library of Congress Control Number: 2018902108

Print information available on the last page.

WestBow Press rev. date: 03/09/2018

I would like to give credit to my friend, Inez Haythorn, for helping me with this book. She has been a friend of the family for years. Her aunt would have me sing "His Eye is on the Sparrow," in church.

Introduction

My name is Duane Clarke, and I would like to tell you the story of my life. I know everyone has a story, but not all people tell their stories. This book is about God, sports, and gambling.

God first, because I give Him all the glory and all the praise. He is first in my life. Next, sports, because from the time I was a youngster, I loved sports. I played baseball, basketball, and football. Then when I was eighteen years old, I became addicted to gambling. Soon I was betting on baseball, basketball, football, poker, horse racing, and dog racing. I ended up having this problem for thirty years, until I was almost forty-eight years old. I will tell you about my parents and the kind of people they were, my childhood, my life as a gambler, my life as the father of four children, and my first wife, who died in 1978 of an aneurysm at the age of thirty-one. I will also tell you about Linda, my wife today. She has been a Christian since she was nineteen years old, and I will tell you how God is so good all the time, as well as how my life has changed since I became a Christian for real. You see, my God is real now. He is real in my heart. I have truly become born again.

The reason why I would like to tell my story is so perhaps others who have addictions will be inspired by my life to give up sin and gain victory over whatever problems they may have. They can live the good life and become the people that God intended them to be. I know we are on this earth for one reason, and that is to serve God, live for God, and live without sin because of the amazing grace God gives us. It is a free gift. I have admitted that I was a sinner, believed that Jesus is the Son of God, and confessed my sins to God.

Wasted Years
by Jimmy Swaggart

Have you lived without
love, a life of tears?
Have you searched for life's
hidden meaning,
Or is your life filled with
long and wasted years?

Wasted years, wasted
years, oh how foolish,
As you walk on in darkness
and in fears;
Turn around, turn around,
God is calling,
He's calling you from a
life of wasted years.

1

Early Years

My mother told me that I was born at 12:17 a.m. on a Saturday. Soon she had me in church. From the time I was born, I was searching for something. I wasn't a typical boy because I couldn't see out of my left eye. I would wonder what was wrong with me.

I wasn't normal like the other children. But at the same time, my life was like being in heaven. My mother and dad took good care of me. I would touch my left eye and wonder why I couldn't see out of it. Other kids could see out of both eyes. Why couldn't I? That is the way God made me.

The first day of school, I was embarrassed because I didn't feel as though I was like the rest of the kids. Now when I look back, I realize I wasn't any different than the other children, though they called me cross-eyed. In today's world, those kids would be considered bullies. I sort of felt like I was in prison with this self-image problem. I was hurt, and I experienced a deep frustration.

At the age of twelve or thirteen, my dad took me to Pittsburgh to see about an operation. The doctor said that the best doctor was in Moundsville, and so we went to the doctor in Moundsville, West Virginia. He operated on me to straighten out my left eye.

My dad and his friend came to the hospital and prayed for me. I had to have a patch over both eyes for a day or so. First, they took the patch off my right eye. Then a week later, the bandage was removed from my left eye. That moment was when I felt as though I had a new beginning in life. I still could not see out of it, but the eye was straight. I felt normal.

God loves me just the way I am. He brought me into the world, and a true friend will like me no matter how I look. Clothing, looks, and possessions don't determine who you are. People need to keep their self-respect and dignity by doing what they know is morally right. Through my life, thinking of others and helping others helped my worth.

My dad once told me that if you go through life and have five good friends, you are blessed. I asked him, "What if you have fifteen good friends?" He replied, "Then you are really blessed."

My parents were great Christian people. There was a lot of love at my house. My dad worked at the glass house for fifty-one years. He provided for his family. He didn't make much money but was still able to raise four children. My dad was also a part-time minister. He became a Christian when he was fourteen years old, and so he was a Christian for most of his life.

He and I would pick up a disabled lady and take her to church. He was very active at church. In the winter he would get up at six in the morning on a Sunday and go down to start the furnace at the church. Sometimes he would clean the snow off of the sidewalk, come back home, and get ready for the service. He was always involved with church work. He read his Bible and prayed. He was paid about twenty-five dollars a week as a part-time minister.

My dad was a very loving person. He always thought of others and was never selfish. Those who really knew my dad knew he was a good, caring man. He stuck to his Christian beliefs no matter what. He lived for God and served God at all times. Dad would not cheat anyone out of a dime. He loved to talk about Jesus.

We would holler for him to come to supper. He wouldn't answer because he would be upstairs with the door shut, praying to God. Lots of days, he would be in the front room reading his Bible. As a very faithful man, my dad loved his children but loved the Lord first.

My dad told me, "You have to live this life as a Christian, loving God and loving others. We are on this earth to serve God." And God truly blessed my parents throughout their lives.

Sometimes I would wonder why he wouldn't let me do a lot of things that other children my age would do. But he knew best. I would ask him for a quarter to go to a movie, and he would ask me what the title was. If he thought it sounded okay, he would give me a quarter.

My mother and dad were married in 1927. They bought a new car in 1927 and then went to Anderson Camp Meeting on their honeymoon. Then they lost the car in the Depression, around 1933.

I have had several people tell me that my parents were true Christians and loving, caring people. My dad was known as an honest man. He would place a box of candy bars in front of the entrance to the glass house where he worked, and he hoped that people would buy one and leave the money in the box. He tried to show people how to be honest. He told me in all those years, he was short only twenty-five cents.

My dad would check his receipt from the store. If they charged him too much, he would tell them. If they didn't charge him enough, he would also tell them. If he owed them ten cents, he would take it back to the store. My dad was a dominant influence in my life.

After my dad passed away, we met a man who owned a Laundromat. He gave us a letter that my dad had sent him.

> The other day I was in your Laundromat, and four extra quarters came out of your machine. I will give them back to you. I always try to be an honest person. God bless you.
>
> Signed,
> Russell Clarke

In God's Word, He tells us to love God first and then our mother, father, and family. I would do anything for them that I could. I try to love God with all my heart, mind, and soul.

> But blessed is the one who trusts in the LORD, whose confidence is in him. (Jeremiah 17:7 NIV)

Dad, in your eyes I've seen God's love. In your words, I've heard His wisdom. Through your life, I've found His grace.

My dad and mom taught me how to love God and one another. There should be no talk of love in the Bible without covering God's love for each of us. This is the love that has led to a path for eternal life.

> Beloved, let us love one another, for love is from God. Whoever loves has been born of God and knows God. (1 John 4:7 KJV)

> For God so loved the world that he gave his one and only Son, that whoever believes in him should not perish but have eternal life. (John 3:16 NIV)

But God demonstrates his own love for us in this: While we were still sinners, Christ died for us. (Romans 5:8 NIV)

Let no debt remain outstanding, except the continuing debt to love one another, for whoever loves others has fulfilled the law. (Romans 13:8 NIV)

Both my parents were faithful to God and family. My mother would play the piano in church, sing solos at church, play for funerals, and sing at weddings. One of her favorite songs to sing was "He Could Have Called Ten Thousand Angels." She could sing like no other.

She would wake me up for school in the morning at 7:15 sharp by playing hymns on the piano. I knew it was time to get up and get ready for school. I didn't need an alarm clock.

My mother was a hardworking mom. She would be down in the basement washing clothes, and in the summertime she would hang the clothes on the outside line to dry.

She would always have our dinner, breakfast, and lunch ready every day. Once a week, we would have chicken, meatloaf, or a roast, and we would sit together at the table.

Peace I leave with you; my peace I give you. I do not give to you as the world gives. Do not let your hearts be troubled and do not be afraid. (John 14:27 NIV)

Even youths grow tired and weary, and young men stumble and fall; but those who hope in the Lord will renew their strength. They will soar on wings like eagles; they will run and not grow weary, they will walk and not be faint. (Isaiah 40:30–31 NIV)

The God of peace will soon crush Satan under your feet. The grace of our Lord Jesus be with you. (Romans 16:20 NIV)

When I was around twelve years old, I would go to church with my parents. I remember one particular Sunday, my dad was up front preaching, and I was in the back with another boy, cutting up. When I got home, my dad told me that I couldn't sit in the back any longer and would have to sit in the front.

I didn't realize at the time, but my parents making me go to church at a young age probably helped me. I wouldn't be the person that I am today if it had not been for my parents. I am glad they dragged me to church. My parents really loved me.

I loved sports. Two of my brothers started me in sports. I would go over about two blocks from my house to play basketball, and the kids in the neighborhood would choose sides and play a baseball game without an umpire. You don't see that today. When I was in grade school, I was a pretty good basketball player and thought I was going to be the next Jerry West. I averaged about seventeen points a game. I would get trophies for playing in grade school. I was pretty good.

As a freshman, I was on the freshman high school varsity basketball team. Around tenth grade football season, I gained a lot of weight and could not play basketball any longer. I played football for three years.

During my sophomore year in high school, I wanted to be a fullback, and the coach didn't agree with that. In practice, the coach told the defense that he was going to call my play eight times in a row. He didn't tell me his plan. My play was called eight times in a row, and the defense hit me hard. On the last one

I got up, and the coach asked if I still wanted to be a fullback. I said, "No, sir," and played on the line, both offense and defense, for two and a half years.

I played football, basketball, and some baseball. My brother took me to a Pirates game when I was around twelve years old. I went to see the Steelers play in the sixties. One year, they had one win and thirteen losses. I went to see the WVU Mountaineer football games for about twenty-five years straight, and I also watched the WVU basketball team.

One Christmas, I wanted a basketball from my parents. That was what I got, and I was very excited. That was all I got, but it was enough.

My favorite players back then were Roberto Clemente, Jerry West, and Jack Lambert. We would go to the Pirates game to watch Roberto Clemente for seventy-five cents. My friend and I would go early to the games at Forbes Field, sit in right field, and get practice baseballs hit to us before the games.

Family

On weekends, my parents would take me on trips to Ohio to visit my uncles, aunts, and cousins. I remember so well that when we went over, we would stop and get ice cream. While coming back, we would stop to get ice cream. We would visit for a day and have a big feast at the table with good homemade food at my aunt's.

When I was about fifteen years old, I attended youth camp at Webster Springs, West Virginia. I had a wonderful time with others my age. The church service was a blessing. I remember coming home, going to the altar, and asking Jesus to come into my heart. Later, I was baptized.

2

Gambling Years

At eighteen years of age, my first job after graduation from high school was delivering groceries for a small grocery store. My first day on the job was the first time I drove a stick shift. The night before, my dad had showed me on a piece of paper how to drive a stick shift. The first day was kind of bumpy.

That day, I went home from work and sat down to read the paper. My mother asked me if I was going to get ready for graduation that night. I was so excited by my first day of work that I forgot. I had my first job and was out of school, living with my parents.

With my earnings from my first job, I bought a 1963 409 engine Chevy Impala. I bought my parents their first color TV set.

Soon came one of the worst days of my life. My brother asked me to go into a local bar and buy Lakers tickets. They were playing at Pittsburgh. I looked up at the board that had the betting line on the basketball games and asked the bartender how that worked. He showed me, and I thought I might like that because I was into sports. The following week, I started betting, and I won two weeks straight. I was hooked. Soon I was betting on basketball, baseball, football, poker, horse racing, and dog racing. My addiction started. I was hooked on gambling at eighteen years old.

I would go into that bar, make my bets, sit in front of the ticker tape to get the scores of the games, and drink beer. I really didn't like beer, but I wanted to be a part of the crowd.

Some of the nights weren't very pleasant; sometimes I would lose my bets and money. One night I had lost my bet and was so mad because I had lost it in the last second of the game. I threw every chair in the bar that was empty. The owner said if I did not quit, he was going to call the police. When I won, everything was okay. But when I lost, what a difference it was.

The owner of the bar would send me and another fellow up to the racetrack to make a bet on certain horses that were sure to win because they were fixed.

I've heard people say they are fixed, and after being around sports all my life, I would say that is true. With horse racing, sometimes it is fixed, and I also believe that some NBA games are fixed.

My gambling problem was so bad that I became very selfish. I didn't care about anything or anybody. All of a sudden, my life was me, me, me. The devil had me exactly where he wanted me.

I had heard on the radio a score of a ballgame in the third quarter. This team was ahead by eight points. I also knew the games must have started at an early time. I went into the bar to make a bet on the game. I thought that I would cheat because the game was not supposed to start till 8:30, but it had started early. They took the bet. I chose the team that was favored by one point, but I knew they were ahead by eight points in the third quarter. I tried to cheat the bookie, but I still lost by the end of the game. The team I bet on lost despite the lead. I wasn't being honest. It was all wrong. I would do anything for money—lie, cheat, steal.

I also remember telling a fellow that I would give him this team, the Buffalo Bills, and fifteen points playing the Steelers on a Sunday afternoon on TV. He said he would take that bet, and we both put our money up. What he didn't know was the game was an exhibition game, and it'd been played the night before. That game was a rerun. I already knew that the Steelers would win by sixteen points, and I was going to win the bet. Again, I tried to cheat and not be honest. Honesty goes out the door when you gamble. You will do anything for money.

I would sometimes sleep only three hours a day because of my gambling problem.

One night, I bet under on a basketball game's total score of both teams with three minutes to go in the game. It looked like I was going to win, and I told everyone in the place that I was going to buy. They needed a combined score of thirty-four points with three minutes to go for me to lose the bet. They went on to score thirty-five points, and I lost the bet.

From age eighteen to twenty-two, my life was working, going to the bars, drinking, gambling, and getting drunk on the weekends. I'd come home late while living with my parents, causing them a lot of problems.

I went from working in a small store to working at a larger grocery chain. I delivered for five stores Monday through Friday and worked at the cash register on Saturdays.

I continued my betting. I forged a check and got in a lot of trouble.

Once, I played poker all afternoon on a Saturday and all night till 6:00 a.m. Sunday morning. There must have been fifteen thousand dollars on the table. We quit playing, and one of the fellows asked me to take him home. While coming back, I ran out of gas. I had around seven hundred dollars on me. Back then, the gas stations were closed up on Sundays, and so I walked home.

I look back on that now and can imagine what my parents went through at that time. I kept it up because I still was into gambling. I would sometimes win, but mostly I lost. Gambling was in my blood.

I treated my parents poorly with my gambling problem. Proverbs 28:24 (NIV) states, "Whoever robs their father or mother and says, 'It's not wrong,' is partner to one who destroys. He is no better than a murderer."

I would gamble with money set aside for something else. It's a bet that no one wins.

Studies show gamblers will go without food and clothes, resorting to theft and other illegal activities to get money for their gambling habit. It is a sin.

A little faith will bring your soul to heaven, but a lot of faith will bring heaven to your soul.

An estimated 80 percent of adult problem gamblers started before age fourteen. A fifteen-year-old girl had an illegal gambling problem. She lost five thousand dollars at a resort even as her father begged the casino to bar her as a minor. Another teenager stole twenty thousand to pay his bookie, and another boy prostituted his girlfriend around school to raise money for his gambling debts. In one state, 90 percent of high school seniors had illegally purchased lottery tickets.

In 1967, I talked my dad into buying a small store. He borrowed money from the bank for me. He must have thought that would help keep me from continuing to gamble. We bought the store on a land contract.

At first, I kept busy running the store, laying off of gambling for a while. One night, my dad came over to the store and said I needed to lower the prices on the bananas before they went bad. I said I didn't think I would. Later, he said it again, and I said okay. I marked them down to ten cents a pound. About ten minutes later, he grabbed a handful of bananas, put them on the counter, and said he would take these. What a sense of humor. Everything was going pretty well. I was making some money—not a lot, but I was paying my bills.

Football season started, and I started gambling again. I had to have action. My life was still all about me. I believed that gambling was a fast way to make money.

I was glad when the weekends would come because the bank wouldn't call me and tell me that I was overdrawn on my checking account.

I was selfish. Psalm 119:36 (NIV) states, "Turn my heart toward your statutes and not toward selfish gain." My heart was in the wrong place. I only cared about selfish gain.

When I was nineteen, a fellow asked me to join the umpires association. I took the test and passed. My first game, I made four dollars and fifty cents. I umpired high school baseball, sandlot games, and little league, pony league, and Legion games.

Another umpire picked me up after work to go down the river to do a Legion game. When I got into the car, he told me that the coach for the home team wanted us to fix the game. He said that the last time they were at the other team's field, the umpire fixed the game for them. I said to myself I was only nineteen years old. I wasn't going to fix a game. Some of the players on the Legion were my age and were a little scared.

In the sixth inning, the score was six to nothing. The home team was winning. I called a balk on the pitcher. I was umpiring the bases, and the umpire behind home plate came out in front of the plate and said, "Clarke, there is no one on base. How could you call a balk?" From that day on, four people told everyone that I fixed the game. But there was no need to fix it anyway, because the home team was winning six to nothing.

I went on to umpire girls' softball, men's softball, and men's fast pitch for twenty-seven years. I told a lot of people that when I quit umpiring, I had the record for the Ohio Valley. I never missed a call in all those years. They were either safe or out, fair ball or foul, a ball or strike. I told Chuck Tanner, the manager of the Pirates. He said that I should have been a major league umpire because they didn't think they missed calls either.

I still had the small grocery store. One day my brother was there, and a lady who lived close to the store came in and bought something. After she left, my brother said to me, "You should ask her out for a date." At the time, I didn't think much of it.

About a month later, I got up enough nerve to call her and ask her out. She did go out with me. Her name was Sheri. She had been married with two children, a three-year-old daughter and a one-year-old son.

She told me that her first husband had been a heavy drinker. We dated for about six months. One fellow called me and said that he was going to ask her out. I said to him, "If she will go out with you, go ahead."

He did ask her out. She said no. After about six months, I asked her to marry me, and she said yes. I look back now and wonder if she would have still married me if I had told her that I had a gambling problem. She probably would have because she was living with her parents, and we were in love. I wish my gambling would have stopped right there. It didn't stop. We were married, ran the store, and rented a house with three bedrooms.

At first, I was very jealous of her kids. She got a job at a local plant, and I was running the store. About a year later, I adopted the kids into the Clarke name, and as the years went by, I truly fell in love with my two kids. I truly loved my wife. I did very little gambling. I was pretty busy with work and family. I was paying the bills.

In 1969, when the high school opened up for the first year,

I got a job as a janitor. My wife quit her job and would work at the store because I would work at night and go home to sleep in the daytime.

At the school, I would work about four hours and sleep in the other four hours. I did not take care of that job very well. About that time, my business went down in the store. I lost the store and lost my job at the high school. My dad went to the bank to pay the payment on the due date, and they said the owner had foreclosed on us. We probably could have fought that, but we didn't because the store business was going down. It was back when there was a store on about every corner. I had been gambling a little at that time.

I started working in Benwood at a chain store that had just opened. I worked there about six weeks before they laid me off. They had hired a lot of extras for when they first opened, and then they laid off eight of us.

We were living in a small apartment with very little money. Around that time in 1969, we had a boy. His name was Duane Allen.

I went up to Ravenna, Ohio, and put in an application to work at a dairy. I started about two weeks later and took my family with me. I was delivering milk house to house in 1970. I didn't make very much money, but I was away from all of that gambling I had done in Moundsville, West Virginia. Soon I got into the bad habit of going to work, coming home, and going about one hour away from where we lived to go to the horse races. I had my wife and three kids living in Newton Fall, Ohio. I would leave them and go down to the racetrack, many times betting with someone else's money. I once again had a gambling problem.

Once, I went down with $650. I lost the first eleven races and had fifty dollars left. I won the last race and came home with $640, ten dollars less than what I'd started with.

I can only imagine what my wife must have felt. She was there by herself with three kids. Her husband would go to work, come home, and leave for the evening. She would go to bed and get up, and her husband would be at work. She was a good wife and didn't deserve this. She had a first husband who was an alcoholic, and now she was married to a gambler. Did I love her and the kids? I couldn't have. I only thought of myself. Where was my love for the family?

> And now these three remain: faith, hope and love. But the greatest of these is love. (1 Corinthians 13:13 NIV)

This went on for about ten months at this dairy, delivering house to house and then doing some gambling. One day I came back from my route, and they told me I was fired because the books were not right.

I went home, told my wife, and went looking for work. I went to give blood so we could have money for food. I tried out a job delivering donuts. A few days later, there was a knock on the door. It was the deputy sheriff arresting me for embezzlement. Friends of mine took my wife and kids back to West Virginia. My children were aged five, three, and one.

As I write this, I am hurting inside and am in tears. How could I have done this? I had a very bad gambling addiction.

The dairy said that I embezzled twelve hundred dollars. I was in jail in Ravenna, Ohio. My dad and two brothers were there to talk to me. My dad told me that he couldn't bail me out. He had done enough to try to help me with my gambling problem. But my two brothers would bail me out and pay back the money.

The judge gave me thirty days in jail, and my family was back in West Virginia living with my parents and my wife's parents.

While in jail, I said to myself, "For God so loved the world that he gave his only begotten Son that whosoever believeth in Him shall not perish but have eternal life" (John 3:16 KJV). I also said God had given me another chance. "When I get out, I am going to quit this gambling and straighten out my life. Not just for me, but also for my family."

After thirty days, I went back to West Virginia and started a new life. But did I? I should have gotten a job that didn't handle money. But I started a new job working for a bakery, delivering house to house in 1971.

We at first rented a house in Wheeling, West Virginia. I also would deliver morning papers before I would go out to deliver bakery goods. I was doing very little gambling. Life was pretty good for my wife and kids at that time.

After about a year, we rented a house on Glen Dale Creek. Then after about six months, we were able to purchase a home out on Route 250 in Moundsville through FHA. It was a new modular home for seventy-five dollars a month. Life was good.

In 1973 we had our fourth child, a boy, Steven Eric. I remember the day he was born. I was delivering bakery goods house to house, and I called to see if my wife was okay. She said she was getting ready to leave to go to the hospital to have the baby, and so I went to the hospital. After our boy was born, I went back to delivering that day.

At that time, we were happy, and things were going well. We went up to Pontiac, Michigan, to visit my brother and had a good time on vacation.

I went to work with the bakery one more year. In 1974, the bakery closed down all routes, and I was again out of work.

While working at the bakery, the hardest time I had was on this one particular route in the winter with a lot of snow on the ground. I was out in the country and would carry about five king-size loaves of bread in one hand and my basket of other goodies in the other. I carried this down a lane about a mile long. I believe I earned my money that day.

About that time, I would go to the bookie and make some small bets on the baseball, basketball, or football seasons. But I did not do anything big.

In 1973, we went to my class's ten-year reunion. I was drinking pretty good, trying to be like the crowd. It had been about five years before that I had quit drinking. By one o'clock in the morning, it took about eight guys to take me home.

We got to our driveway. They asked my wife, "Where do you want him?"

She said, "Leave him in the car."

I woke up Sunday afternoon pretty sick. That was the last time that I was drunk, the last time I would drink any beer.

When I was out of work, I worked for a dry-cleaning company, picking up clothes and delivering house to house for about five months.

A few weeks later, I was able to get a job delivering for a milk company. That was a mistake. It was 1974, and I would collect money from the customers. Some would send their bills into the dairy. I was handling money once again that did not belong to me.

I remember my wife telling a friend of hers that she was glad she'd married me because her life was a lot better now.

I told my wife that I was going up to the racetrack to bet on this one horse that I thought was going to win. The horse won, and I won $150. I came back home. I still had gambling in my blood.

I told my eye doctor about my gambling problem. She asked me how she could keep her kids from starting to gamble. I thought of when I first went into that bar and started running around with the wrong crowd. I told her to make sure she didn't let her kids run around with the wrong people.

Things were going pretty well about that time. My daughter was in the fourth grade, my oldest son was in second grade, my middle son was kindergarten, and my youngest son was about two years old. I would take my wife down to her parents' about two times per week; she didn't drive. I was working long hours at the dairy. I would get home at five or six o'clock, go to bed around nine, and get up at five to go to work.

When the children were a little older, the two oldest were in the junior high band. The oldest boy played some little league baseball. When the other two were older, they played baseball, and I coached them for about six years. Sometimes I would get home from work just in time to go to the games.

I would visit my parents and my wife's parents. I would take my wife places. Her parents were very good people. If only I hadn't had that gambling problem.

My wife went to a revival at our church and was saved and baptized. I didn't go that night. My parents wanted me to go, but I didn't.

In mid-seventies, I took the family up to a Pirates ball game. As we were going to our seats, a fellow asked me if I wanted to take the family to a luxury box. We did, and while we had a good time watching the game, my wife read a book. It was nothing for my wife to read a book in a couple of days. She would read a lot of Harlequin romance books. My wife was a good lady. I didn't treat her as well as I should have because of my gambling addiction.

Ladies, this is a good man:

* He will love you just the way you are. He will accept your kids as if they were his own. When I first married her, I will admit that I didn't treat her two kids like my own.

But as they got older, I believe I did. I had my ups and downs with them, but I grew to love them very much. To this day, I would do anything for them. I love all my children very much.

- He will be sensitive to your needs.
- He will spend time with you.
- He will pray with you and for you.
- He will make sure your home is safe.
- He will help you financially.
- He will not lie or cheat on you.
- He will appreciate your intelligence.
- He will be proud of your accomplishments.
- He will encourage you.
- He will build you up and not tear you down.
- He will never disrespect you.

I wasn't a very good man back then. I wasn't a very good father.

I continued to pocket some money that didn't belong to me. It was a miracle that I didn't get caught at it. One would have thought that after all I had been through, I would not have done that. I had been in jail from it, forged checks, and caused my parents all kinds of problems.

I came up short several times on my route, but they would take it out of my paycheck. One day the amount was six hundred dollars. I was called into the office. They said that I was short a lot, and they heard I was into gambling. I denied it. It was truly a miracle that I was not put in jail again, but I wasn't. About that time, I was delivering a lot of pints of milk not only to houses but also to the plants and filling stations in the area.

In early 1978, I went on a five-day vacation to New York with eight fellows. We were going to the NIT basketball tournaments at Madison Square Garden. One of the fellows whom I went with was my bookie. I was able to make my bets on the games. I took about seventeen hundred dollars with me and came home broke. One fellow wanted to bet on everything: whether a player would make a foul shot or not, or whether a team would make a certain amount of points in the last three minutes. I remember my wife saying that I had gambling pretty bad when I would bet on two ants crawling across the floor and which one would get there first. That is a pretty bad problem.

I left my family back home for five days. A gambler has to have action and will do anything to get money for his problem. New York is definitely Sin City. When I got back from New York, I said that I was back home where people were more down to earth.

ESPN came out with a movie about a well-known baseball player who had a gambling problem. It showed when he was managing baseball. It showed him in his office, giving his bets to his runner on the games and then making his bets. It showed him in the dugout looking over to see whether his runner was back in his seat. Then when he would be back in his seat, that would mean that the fellow would have all his bets in. He would feel a lot better when having in his bets.

When you are into gambling, you have to have action all the time. Then you feel better inside. A gambler thinks he is always going to win, but he ends up losing more than he wins.

In September 1978, my wife woke me to take the family out to St. Clairsville and have a family picture taken. We did have that picture taken. My daughter at that time was thirteen, my oldest son was eleven, the next son was nine, and the youngest son was five. At this time in my life, something was about to happen that would change my and my children's lives.

I went to work on a Tuesday. On that day, I had to stop for

road construction for about a half hour going to my stop and coming back. That made me get back to the dairy late. When I pulled in to unload and load, the fellow told me not to do anything with my truck. He said I needed to go over to the hospital because my wife was there.

When I got to the hospital, my wife's family was there. They told me that she'd passed out at about 3:30. Somehow, she was able to call the neighbor lady. They rushed her in the ambulance to the hospital. As they were taking my wife out of the lane, the kids were coming off the bus and heading down the lane from the hospital. Can you imagine what was going through their minds while their mom was in an ambulance and going to the hospital.

When I got to the hospital, my wife was in a coma. We were all very upset. Several doctors tried to figure out what was wrong with her and what had happened. This went on for a couple days. On Friday night, the doctor called me into the room and showed me that she'd had an aneurysm in her brain, and that there was nothing he could do. I asked him, "If I had brought her to you a year ago, would you have found out the problem?"

He answered, "No. This is something that could have started when she was born and then burst open at that time."

I remember that I would take her to the doctor with a headache, and they couldn't find anything wrong with her.

A nurse gave me a penny with a Bible verse, John 3:16. The nurse told me that she loved me and that God loved me. That did give me some comfort.

On Saturday morning, the doctor told me I needed to start thinking about pulling the plug on her. I talked to the family, and they agreed that I should do it. The family brought the children up to the hospital to see their mother for the last time. With a lot of tears shed, I went into her room on Sunday. I told her that I would see her in heaven, and we pulled the plug. That was a very hard thing to do. She died at 12:00 p.m. on that Sunday. Then I went down to the in-laws and told the kids. The oldest son stood up and said, "We can still be a family."

> For me, to live is Christ and to die is gain. (Philippians 1:21 NIV)

> Then I heard a voice from heaven say, "Write this: Blessed are the dead who die in the Lord from now on."

> "Yes," says the Spirit, "they will rest from their labor, for their deeds will follow them." (Revelation 14:13 NIV)

> Precious in the sight of the LORD is the death of his saints. (Psalm 116:15 KJV)

Believers belong to the Lord in heaven.

> Jesus said to her, "I am the resurrection and the life. The one who believes in me will live, even though they die; and whoever lives by believing in me will never die." (John 11:25–26 NIV)

Believers receive an eternal inheritance in heaven. But we must be born again.)

On the day of the showing in the funeral home, my youngest son stood by me, holding on to my leg. When I cried, he also cried.

Life went on. The kids went back to school, except my youngest didn't want to go. I told him that I was going to take him down to the police station. I left him sitting in the car and went around the corner with my eye on him. I stood there for about two minutes, and then went back to the car and told him that they would have to come out to the house and talk to him if he didn't go to school. He went to school. I really didn't want to do that, but I had to do something to get him in school.

About two months after my wife died, I went to the post office and picked up the family picture that we had taken two months before she'd died. It was very tough when I saw that picture.

The first year, we had one babysitter. In about one year, I sold the house, and we moved to Moundsville, about three miles from where we had lived in the country. I made eleven thousand dollars, and that was probably my downfall again with my gambling problem.

I continued to gamble. I made a bet on the Super Bowl of 1979. The Steelers were favored by three and a half points, and the over and under was thirty-seven. I called, and the bookie told me that line was three and a half, and I had won a bet the night before. I should have said to give me Pittsburgh and over, but I didn't. I waited till fifteen minutes before the game and called him. He said the line went up to four and a half. I told him to give me Pittsburgh and at four and a half over thirty-seven. Why I did not bet on the game when the line was three and a half was beyond me. With about six minutes to go, the score was 35–17 Steelers. I told the boys that I was going to win a big bet. Then the Steelers went into the prevent defense, and I lost. The final score was Steelers 35, Cowboys 31. The Cowboys scored two touchdowns. Then I was back into gambling again.

Living in town made it easier to get babysitters. I told my daughter that she could go to her friend's for one night, but the other nights she had to stay home with the boys. It was tough for my daughter, living with me and her brothers. My daughter was in the band at that time, and the oldest son was in middle school band. He also played some first base in the little league, and the two youngest boys were playing baseball.

I would continue to take them to Pirates games, WVU football and basketball games, and high school basketball games.

About four years after my wife died, I tried going back to church, but that didn't do me much good. I was down to about five thousand dollars left, and I was going to buy a car for that price. But I didn't. It burned a hole in my pocket, and I continued to gamble it away. When I first sold the house, I should have bought a house, but I continued to rent.

From 1981 to 1991

It was around 1981 or 1982. My youngest son was around eight years old. My middle son and I got into an argument. My youngest son ran upstairs, crying. Then he finally settled down to a nap. When he woke up, he wrote me a short letter. In the letter he said, "Dad, why did we have to lose our mother? I know running away would not do me any good. I know I love you and wish you could get us another mother. Life would be a lot better. I'm going to try to love everybody more, keep practicing my sports, and loving you and my sister and brothers. I love you. Steve."

I believe at that time, he didn't know which way to turn. He was confused and heartbroken. What a wonderful son he is today. All my children are wonderful today.

My daughter graduated from high school and went on to become a nurse. While she was in college, she was staying with her grandma. I believe she'd had about enough of her dad and brothers. That was understandable!

My oldest son was in the tenth grade. The band would go on band competitions. One year I went to Tennessee with them as a chaperone. There were ninety-six bands and eight hours of music.

I did not think I would like that, but I did. John Marshall came in nineteenth overall in the competition. I worked afternoons and had very little chance to do something like this. It was a fun trip. It was good getting away from working and gambling on ball games.

My oldest son graduated from high school in 1985. I still wasn't as close to my children as I should have been. My middle son played football in the tenth, eleventh, and twelfth grades. He loved sports and played some baseball in the little league and colt league. He graduated in 1989.

My youngest son was about nine years old in 1982. From then through 1991, he was involved in school and sports. He came home from a ninth grade dance, and I asked him if he had fun. He answered, "No. I could have been out there playing basketball." He loved to play basketball. He was the point guard on the high school team in his tenth, eleventh, and twelfth years of high school. He also was the quarterback on the football team and played baseball his eleventh and twelfth grades. He graduated in 1991 from high school.

In 1986 I had a carpal tunnel operation on both hands and was off work for six months, drawing compensation. I wasn't working and did a little gambling till I ran out of money. Then I would wait until I received my next comp check.

From 1981 to 1991, while my kids were going through school, playing sports, and participating in the band, I was working mostly the afternoon shift at the dairy. I would go to the bookie place and bet on sports year-round. I would tell my parents that I wasn't gambling any longer. My parents sold their house and went into a high-rise. After a couple of years, my mother had to be put in a home with physical problems. My dad quit driving in about 1984. That just about killed him.

Around that time, I went on another gambling trip to New

York for about four days. I left with around eighteen hundred dollars. I won some and came home with around two thousand dollars. I had won that time. I would go to the bookie, sit there, and say to myself, "What am I doing here? Why am I like this?" I didn't have many true friends. I wasn't a friend to others like I should have been. I was still a very selfish person.

For men shall be lovers of their own selves, covetous, boasters, proud, blasphemers, disobedient to parents, unthankful, unholy, without natural affection, trucebreakers, false accusers, incontinent, fierce, despisers of those that are good, traitors, heady, high minded, lovers of pleasures more than lovers of God. (2 Timothy 3:2–4 KJV)

> For all seek their own, not the things which are Jesus Christ's. (Philippians 2:21 KJV)
>
> We then that are strong ought to bear the infirmities of the weak and not to please ourselves. (Romans 15:1 KJV)

My life was all about me, me, me. My children had to take care of themselves. People will say to me today that I did a pretty good job raising my children. I didn't, because they pretty much had to raise themselves without a mother—and without a dad too. Yes, I would give them money for school, take them to ball games, and go watch their games when I could, but the way I worked and was into my own life, I didn't do a very good job.

Around 1986, I put myself in a hospital in Clay, Georgia, for twenty-nine days for overeating and gambling. My youngest son was around thirteen and playing eighth or ninth grade football. My middle son was about seventeen and in the tenth grade, playing football for John Marshall. My oldest son was one year out of school. My daughter got married in 1986 or 1987.

I left the boys by themselves and went in that hospital in Clay, Georgia, on one day's notice. While in the hospital, I did lose twenty-six pounds, but the doctor said that he thought I had more of a gambling problem than I did an overeater's problem. The doctor gave me an IQ test and told me the next day that I'd scored a ninety-nine on it. I could still live a normal life. The fact was I didn't think I was living a normal life. The doctor also told me that when I got up the next morning and took my walk, he wanted me to say to the first person I ran in to that my name was Duane Clarke and that I was a loser.

I did that. At the first person I ran into, I said, "My name is Duane Clarke, and I am a loser." You should have seen the look on his face.

That afternoon, the doctor asked me if I'd done it and how it felt. I answered him by saying, "I am not a loser, but if I continue to live this way, I will always be a loser in life because of the way I have lived."

We would meet every afternoon for meetings, and the counselor asked me if I would, as an assignment, write my wife (who had died about nine years before that) a letter. We were to read it on the following Tuesday. That gave me the weekend to write the letter.

On that Tuesday afternoon, I read the letter to about twelve people in the class.

Dear Sheri,

> In writing this letter to you at Woodridge Hospital, Georgia, Sunday, August 23, 1987, you could find me sad, hurt, and angry with myself. It's sad to think the hurt I caused you when you were alive. I'm angry with myself to think the way I threw my life away, especially when you were

alive. I'm sad with myself at the way I hurt your children and mine.

Let us start back on our wedding day. I was one happy person. We were close and were friends. You were loving, tender, passionate, and warm. But something happened along the way. I got jealous, bitter, stubborn, and most of all confused.

I became isolated with myself in my own way. I was a confused person. I continued with my gambling. I thought I loved you, and I did, but it was the wrong kind of love.

I owned that store where we met each other. We lost it because of my gambling. Then we moved to Ohio and worked for the milk company. I think back to when I used to leave you and the children to drive seventy miles to the racetrack. How could I have done that? How did you stick with me through thick and thin?

I spent thirty days in jail, and you were waiting on me when I got out. Then our marriage became somewhat better when we bought the house. We had some good times together, but my life was still confused. I can feel the pain I caused you. I can feel the suffering I caused you. From my gambling, I can feel the hurt. I was so stubborn when I wanted to watch ballgames on the television just because I had a bet on the game.

You would like to do things like visit your mother, and I would be very stubborn. I am very sorry that I didn't take you to your mother's two days before you went into a coma. I have felt the pain in my heart since you passed on to live with God.

I accepted God in my life about five years ago, but I was still confused. I thought God was going to perform miracles, I suppose. But one day, I was at my lowest in life, about ready to fall off a cliff. I said I was sick of this. I watched an ad on TV about Woodridge Hospital. Since I have been here, I have found out that I was sick, that I was an compulsive gambler and eater. I have a disease.

I have started to find out the reason that I was angry, sad, and hurt, and how I had hurt you and the children. I went to church this morning and felt the presence of God. Right now, I feel happy that I am learning about myself. I feel I am going to take the possible steps I need to take to live the life I know how to live. How joyous a life a person can live. I will have a long road to travel, but with the help of God, I know I will make it.

From this day on, I will make a promise to me, to God, and to you. I will take one day at a time, and I will love my children and yours the way God would want.

Sheri, I am so sorry. But I know now that it wasn't my fault that I had a disease. Sheri, I remember that the last words I said to you when you passed on: "I love you and will see you in heaven.

Now I can say it to you with meaning. I love you and will see you in heaven.

Love,
Duane

I came back from Woodridge and somewhat settled down. I went back to work. My daughter, Sonya, was out of college and was married to a good man. My oldest son, Noel, graduated from high school, went to work in New Jersey, and later lived in Dravosburg, Pittsburgh, for a year or two.

In 1988, my middle son played football on the high school team. My youngest son was a sophomore and played basketball and football that year. The coach let my middle son play fullback the last game of his senior year. My youngest son handed off to him, and he scored a touchdown! For me, that was something to see.

Around that time, I was working and was into gambling only a little. I went to all the games the boys were in. I did not know that God had a plan in my life that was going to happen about four years later.

When my youngest son graduated from high school, I weighed my highest 412 pounds. I think I put myself under a lot of stress after Sheri had died, and I was going to the icebox a lot.

Around 1990 or 1991, I received a check in the mail that was from the insurance company. It was to be paid to a doctor. The check was for eleven hundred dollars. Instead of paying the bill to the doctor, I started back into gambling big-time. I went to the bookie and started betting again on football, basketball, and baseball. At first I would win often, and I seemed to have money all the time. My oldest son was working and was in and out of the house. My middle son was working after he graduated from high school, and my youngest son graduated in 1991 and then went to college. Things were normal. But was I living a normal life by living the way God would have wanted me to live? I was still living in sin. With my job, I hadn't been working a route for about ten years, so that I couldn't take money that didn't belong to me.

At about that time, I would visit my dad, where he lived in the Towers, and my mom was in a nursing home. The doctor said my mother probably would have to stay in the home for the rest of her life. In 1991, she was able to go back down to the Towers and live with Dad for about a year. Then she had to go back into the home.

I would go to church once in a while, but not steadily. Mom and Dad would not always make it to church. My dad was eighty-one or eighty-two, and Mom was seventy-six.

One or two years later, on Saturday, February 26, I went down to my dad's, and our minister was there. My dad said, "I just wish the good Lord would take me home."

The following Wednesday morning, I had just got home from working at midnight and gone to bed. The phone rang. My brother told me that Dad was in the hospital; they think he had a stroke. I went to the hospital and stayed there for a couple of hours. They told me that I needed to go home and get some sleep because there wasn't much I could do.

I did so for about five hours. When I got up, I had to go to the sports bar and make a bet. I passed the hospital on my way home. Instead of stopping by the hospital to see how my dad was, I drove home. I was still a very selfish person. When I got home, I received a phone call from the hospital saying that I should come at once.

I went to the hospital and was there for about a half hour when they came in and told us that my dad had died. He died on March 4, 1992. This was a very important date in my life, and I will never forget it.

Three days later was the funeral. I had to go to the sports bar to collect my winnings from the night before—and to make a bet—before I went to my dad's funeral. At that time I was betting pretty and winning pretty well. Sad, isn't it, to think that I had to do this before I went to my dad's funeral? After my dad died, I went on with my life, betting on games. At that season, it would have been basketball games.

My dad found an article about gambling in our church magazine. The magazine was called *The Gospel Trumpet*. He was trying anything he could to help me. Here is a quote from the article, which was in the February 6, 1930, issue:

> But in gambling, the one who loses, even though he may be a good sport, is always harmed. And the transferee, or the man who acquires wealth in this way, while he may be the gainer materially, loses spiritually and morally, and the material gain is not to be compared in any respect to the moral and spiritual loss.

Some Nasty Facts about Gambling

Today, people are going bankrupt or committing suicide because of the consequences of their gambling. For example, a person may win $1,500 at a casino. He collects the money when he leaves and must sign for it. But let's say that he decides to take this money, go back inside, and gamble with it—but this time lose it. His winnings has already been recorded, and at the end of the year, he has to pay taxes on it, even though he lost the money shortly after winning it. This is why many gamblers go bankrupt.

For every $88,000 a poker machine takes in, only $6,000 of that is actually paid out.

3

A Life Redeemed

From the day my dad died, I started having a heavy heart about the way I had treated my dad and mother with my gambling problem. I caused them a lot of heartache. My parents had prayed for me for around thirty years. About five weeks after dad had died, on April 11, 1992, I asked Jesus to forgive my sins. "I am sick and tired of being sick and tired. Please come into my heart. I want to live for you, Jesus. You died on the cross for me for my sins, and I know you will wipe them all away, all forgotten from that day on."

Jesus said, "Go and sin no more. Your sins are forgiven." I will start a new life in Christ. Read my Bible and live for you.

About three days later, I went to get some gas in my car and bought four lottery tickets. Then I said, "What am I doing? I just got saved for real." From that day on, I haven't gambled—not even a lottery ticket. I had been gambling for about thirty years.

I received the Holy Spirit on April 11, 1992, and was born again. Two months after April 11, I had a knock at my front door. The landlord wanted to know if I wanted to buy the house. It had an apartment on the back of the house. He had remodeled it and had planned to live in it. But he had just gotten married again and was going to move out of town. He said he would sell it to me on a land contract. So I did. In 1992, I didn't realize at the time, but God was blessing me. I believe when you get saved for real, God sees your heart and knows you mean business, and He blesses you. I believe.

I used to pay a guy a hundred to pick winners for me. I wouldn't have really needed to because I could pick them as well as he could. But a year after I became a Christian, an interesting thing happened. The man called me and asked me why I hadn't been in contact with him. To his surprise, I told him that I didn't gamble anymore. He asked, "Then what are you doing for fun?"

I answered, "I am going to church!"

He hung up on me. He saw that he could no longer make money from me.

Then about ten months later, God blessed me with a new wife, Linda. She had been a Christian since she was nineteen years old. The day we were married, I couldn't stop crying. I felt so blessed to be marrying again, fourteen years after my first wife had died. I felt so at peace with myself. I felt loved by the God of the universe. Praise His holy name! I have felt closer and closer each passing day.

God has continued to bless us both. In the year 2000, I had a stroke and went back to work about three months later. Then I hurt my back at work and had to retire at fifty-seven years old. I stepped out of that job with a lot of faith, believing that God would take care of me because I was only going to retire at five hundred dollars a month. Then I was able to draw social security disability about a year later.

I fought with Ohio State Compensation for about three years before I got paid state compensation. They had sent me to a doctor, and he told me that I couldn't work; he would send the letter to the state compensation. He lied to me and then told them that I could work light duty. I remember when I received that doctor report, it was on a Wednesday, and I was pretty upset. I went to prayer meeting and prayed about it. I came back home and prayed till two o'clock in the morning. I told God that I was going to put it into his hands and step out in faith that I would get my state compensation. About six months later, I heard from my lawyer that I'd won my case, and I should come over to the office to get my check. He said that I would receive two checks a month for the rest of my life. Another blessing! God is good all the time!

In 2004, I had colon cancer surgery followed by twenty-four treatments, and today I am cancer-free. Another blessing! In 2010, I had a hernia operation. I had what looked like a volleyball sticking out of my stomach. The doctor told me before he would operate on me, I had to lose weight. I lost 116 pounds. He operated on me in Cleveland, Ohio. The day of the operation, I was okay, but the next day I had several complications: shortness of breath, kidney failure, two spots on my lungs, high sugar, high blood pressure, and trouble breathing. They gave me two blood transfusions. My family, friends, and the church prayed for me for five days.

I had people in Arizona and in Florida praying for me. I know without a doubt that God took care of me, and I was able to go home in about six days. God continues to bless me and my wife to this day.

In the year 2000, my wife had cancer of the throat. She was operated on, and the doctors scraped some of her vocal cords. She couldn't talk; for a year, she whispered. We were told that there was a doctor in Morgantown who could operate. He put an implant to close on her vocal cord, and she could talk again. Praise the Lord! God is good! We were blessed!

I know that when God sees you mean business when you

turn your life over to Him and become born again, He blesses you. He sure did for me and my wife. I love Him so much, and I love my wife.

> But blessed is the one who trusts in the Lord, whose confidence is in him. They will be like a tree planted by the water that sends out its roots by the stream. It does not fear when heat comes. Its leaves are always green. It has no worries in a year of drought and never fails to bear fruit. (Jeremiah 17:7–8 NIV)

> May he give you the desires of your heart and make all your plans succeed. (Psalm 20:4)

> "For I know the plans I have for you," declares the Lord, "plans to prosper you and not to harm you, plans to give you hope and a future." (Jeremiah 29:11 NIV)

> And my God will meet all your needs according to the riches of his glory in Christ Jesus. (Philippians 4:19 NIV)

> The Lord is my shepherd, I lack nothing. He makes me lie down in green pastures, he leads me beside quiet waters. (Psalm 23:1–2 NIV)

The ABCs of Beginning a Relationship with God

The day I became a Christian was the day I started a relationship with God.

Acknowledge

Acknowledge that the Bible is true when it says that you are a sinner disconnected from God and in need of a Savior. "For all have sinned and fall short of the glory of God" (Romans 3:23 NIV).

Surely the arm of the Lord is not too short to save, nor his ear too dull to hear. But your iniquities have separated you from your God; your sins have hidden his face from you, so that he will not hear. (Isaiah 59:1–2 NIV)

For the wages of sin is death, but the gift of God is eternal life in Christ Jesus our Lord. (Romans 6:23 NIV)

Believe

Believe Jesus is who He said He is, and that He can save you right now.

> Yet to all who did receive him, to those who believed in his name, he gave the right to become children of God—children born not of natural descent, nor of human decision or a husband's will, but born of God. (John 1:12–13 NIV)

Confess

> If you declare with your mouth, "Jesus is Lord," and believe in your heart that God raised him from the dead, you will be saved. For it is with your heart that you believe and are justified, and it is with your mouth that you profess your faith and are saved. (Romans 10:9–10 NIV)

Call

Call upon God to save you. Commit your life to him now by repenting of sin and surrendering to Jesus' leadership as Lord of your life. Continue to make that choice daily. Anyone who calls on the name of the Lord will be saved. (Romans 10:13)

For Christ's love compels us, because we are convinced that one died for all, and therefore all died. And he died for all, that those who live should no longer live for themselves but for him who died for them and was raised again. (2 Corinthians 5:14–15 NIV)

Determine

Determine to begin doing everything He says. Devote the rest of your life to developing and nurturing your personal love relationship with Him. Learn the difference between knowing about God and truly knowing God by experience.

Jesus replied, "'Love the Lord your God with all your heart and with all your soul and with all your mind.' This is the first and greatest commandment." (Matthew 22:37–38 NIV)

If you love me, keep my commands. (John 14:15 NIV)

If you keep my commands, you will remain in my love, just as I have kept my Father's commands and remain in his love. (John 15:10 NIV)

> Now this is eternal life: that they know you, the
> only true God, and Jesus Christ, whom you have
> sent. (John 17:3 NIV)

Family

I never did forget the day I had told my children that their
mother had passed. My oldest son stood up and said we could still
be a family. He was eleven years old at the time.

One person said maybe I should have adopted them out. In
all my selfishness, I knew I couldn't do that. Down deep in my
heart, I wouldn't and couldn't do that. Now, today we have unity
in our family. The is exactly what the world needs.

My daughter is a nurse today (a very good one), and she's a
family person. My oldest son is a fire chief. He is a good person
and does a lot for his community. My middle son is a manager at
a mission barbecue restaurant; they give to the community and
give to firemen and police families. My youngest son is a high
school principal. We have kept the family together, and I am very
proud of them. We are still family. I believe they all take God
with them every day.

> And now these three remain: faith, hope and love.
> But the greatest of these is love. (1 Corinthians
> 13:13 NIV)

Nothing is more important than God and family.

Linda is a precious gift given to me by God. Thank you, Jesus!
I know that God brought her to me. God is a wonderful God. I
know that God has changed my heart. I love my wife today and
forever. Thank You, Jesus. Jesus is the center of our marriage. A
few months ago, I said to Linda that we need to start watching
what we say to each other, and we need to start praying together.

We did, and life is a lot better now. We both feel closer to God and each other.

A real man never hurts a woman. Be very careful when you make a woman cry, because God counts her tears. A woman came out of a man's rib. Not from his feet to be walked on, and not from his head to be superior. But from his side to be equal, under the arm to be protected, and next to his heart to be loved.

I made some bad choices in my life. But on April 11, 1992, I made the right one, and I also know that Jesus is the only way and the right one to make.

Jesus is the Way to the Father. (John 14:)

Do not let your hearts be troubled. You believe in God; believe also in me. My Father's house has many rooms; if that were not so, would I have told you that I am going there to prepare a place for you? And if I go and prepare a place for you, I will come back and take you to be with me that you also may be where I am. You know the way to the place where I am going. (John 14:1–4 NIV)

I am the way and the truth and the life. No one comes to the Father except through me. (John 14:6 NIV)

God gives hope to our troubled hearts. Have you ever felt troubled and uncertain about your future? Have you ever felt God was unaware of your world turning upside down? The disciples may have been experiencing these feelings when Jesus gave this message. He had just told them that He was going to leave them, and they were extremely concerned. Yet He tells them not to be troubled and gives them three reasons why they should have peace in their hearts.

1. We can take God at His word. Jesus said, "Trust in God and trust also in me." He was reminding his disciples to trust in God's Word. Scripture has spoken of both Jesus's impending crucifixion and resurrection. Somehow they had missed that. Sometimes we forget to look at the whole picture when our circumstances seem overwhelming. But we must remember that the words found in the Bible will never disappear (Matthew 24:35).

2. We are going to heaven. The next time you face some kind of difficulty, be it physical, emotional, or spiritual, put it in perspective. Remember that you are going to heaven. Your trials are only temporary. When you're in the presence of the Lord, there will be no more fear, death, pain, or sorrow.

3. Jesus is coming back for us. Notice that Jesus says, "I will come and get you." The Lord is not merely going to send for us. He is going to personally escort us to the Father's house. The Bible tells us to encourage each other with these words (1 Thessalonians 4:18). In the midst of your trials, remember that God cares for you so much that He is coming back so that you can be with Him forever. God did not create us for time. He created us for eternity.

We have a lot of choices to make in life, but there are only two to make for eternity: heaven or hell. I am so glad I made two right choices twenty-two years ago on April 11, 1992. I am so glad I am a part of the family of God.

We Can Still Be a Family

There are three things that last: faith, hope, and love. The greatest of these is love.

Faith: My parents had a lot of faith in God, believing that God would bring me to my feet and that someday that I would accept Him as Lord and Savior and of my life. They prayed a lot for me and my family.

Hope: My parents had hope that someday I would accept the Lord and Savior and be in heaven with them.

Love: This is the greatest of these.

Although my parents would say no to me a few times, it was because they knew best for me. They wanted to teach me good values such as honesty, and they wanted me to love everyone with all my heart. I truly believe that my parents taught me to do this—to love God and love one others.

I now read my Bible, pray, and learn more each day about life. I once asked a minister, "Why is it so hard to understand God's Word?" He said to me, "When you read the Bible, listen to God and what He is telling you. Know from it what is right and wrong, and apply it to your life."

My faith and hope for my children is that they have a lot of love in their hearts.

Lord, help me to live from day to day in such a self-forgetful way so that even when I kneel to pray, my prayers shall be for others. Yes, others. Let that be my motto.

Because He lives, I can face tomorrow. Because He lives, all fear is gone. Because I know He holds the future, and life is worth living simply because He lives.

> I was sinking deep in sin, far from the peaceful shore. Very deeply stained with sin, sinking to rise no more. But the Master of the sea heard my despairing cry.

From the waters lifted me, now safe am I. Love lifted me. Love lifted me. When nothing else could help, love lifted me. (James Rowe 1912)

This is my story. This is my song. Praising my Savior all the day long. (Frances J. Crosby 1873)

How can I judge people anymore in my life? Those without sin cast the first stone.

When I fall, He catches me. When I am sad, He holds me. When I cry, He wipes my tears. When I am broken, He puts me back together. My Savior. (Unknown)

Knowing and trusting God is the source of inexpressible joy. The greatest joy we can experience comes only from a personal relationship with Jesus Christ (1 Peter 1:8). Thanks be to our Lord Jesus Christ.

There is a song I learned in Sunday school a long time ago. It says something along the lines of, "Jesus loves the little children of the world." So if Christians are trying to emulate Christ, shouldn't we love people, who are God's children regardless of race, creed, or even sexual orientation?

God, I trust You with all of my heart. Wherever You want me to go I will go, even if it's not where I planned. Lead me, and I will follow. God has worked lots of miracles in my life.

One day, everyone is going to face eternity. You can never run far enough to escape the penalty of sin. No one can hide from almighty God. But the good news is you can always turn around and run back to Him. He is always ready to receive us back with open arms, and He desires to forgive our sins. All we have to do is turn from our sin, put our faith to work, and trust in His Son, Jesus Christ.

I stopped running from God on April 11, 1992. I surrendered my life to him, and I am thankful every day that I did.

1. The Holy Spirit comforts us.
2. The Holy Spirit convicts us of wrongdoing.
3. The Holy Spirit enables us to obey God.
4. The Holy Spirit teaches and guides us.
5. The Holy Spirit gives us power.
6. The Holy Spirit helps us to pray.

We will never change the world by going to church. We will only change the world by being the church. We will change the world by following the early Christians' belief in caring for others as Jesus preached, without a church.

I am redeemed. Dear Lord, into Your hands I place my worries, cares, and troubles. Into Your wisdom I place my path, direction, and my goal. Into Your love I place my life.

Don't give up on God. He never gives up on you. Jesus didn't say, "Follow Christians." He said, "Follow me." God's plan for your life far exceeds the circumstances of your day.

Life is too short to argue and fight with the past. Count your blessings. Value your life and move on with your head held high.

Heavenly Father, I may not understand how everything will work out. But I trust You. I don't see a way. I have faith that at this very moment, You are touching hearts, opening doors, and lining up the right breaks and opportunities. Things look dark and black now, but I have faith that my dream is coming. In Jesus's name, amen.

God tells us to burden Him with whatever burdens us. "The righteous person may have many troubles, but the Lord delivers him from them all" (Psalm 34:19 NIV).

Sports are temporary. Jesus is forever.

> His eye is on the sparrow. And I know He watches
> me. (Civilia D. Martin 1905)

Yes, grace is amazing. Each moment in life is precious. My living shall not be in vain. I believed.

> Fools give full vent to their rage, but the wise
> bring calm in the end. (Proverbs 29:11 NIV)

It's not a sin to get angry. Even Jesus got angry at times. It's what we do with our anger that makes all the difference in the world. Will Rogers said, "People who fly into a rage always make a bad landing."

It amazes me when I look out into the ocean, see God's beauty, and think how small a person I am. I think about how God loved me so much that He came to the earth as a man, and then He died on a cross for me so that my sins could be forgiven. Simply by my asking Him to forgive me of my sins, He saved my soul. Praise the Lord a million times over and over.

> Be completely humble and gentle. Be patient,
> bearing with one another in love. Make every
> effort to keep the unity of the Spirit through the
> bond of peace. (Ephesians 4:2 NIV)

> Peter replied, "Repent and be baptized, every
> one of you, in the name of Jesus Christ for the
> forgiveness of your sins. And you will receive the
> gift of the Holy Spirit." (Acts 2:38 NIV)

God doesn't scare them. They don't fear God. But when they

die, who is going to judge them? Not the devil, and not their spouse. God is to judge all of us as to how we lived this life. The God of the universe is the God who made us all.

A Letter to My Dad in Heaven

I look back in my life. You raised me the way that I should have been raised. You loved me, took good care of me, and provided for me. You raised me the way God would have wanted you to, in a wonderful Christian home.

The worst day of my life was when I walked into that bar and started a thirty-year gambling problem. I became selfish and lived in sin big-time. You tried to help many times when I was in my trouble. God gave me a wonderful wife and four lovely children, and you tried to help me with my family.

I didn't love you like I should have, but you sure loved me. When I was in jail, and you told me that you couldn't help me any longer, that was the right thing for you to do. But my two brothers did help me get out of jail. I still continued to gamble, and I hurt you many times, over and over again.

Right now, as I write this letter to you, I am still hurting inside because of how I treated you with my gambling problem. The day you died and went to heaven, I started to hurt inside because of how I treated you.

Five weeks later, I gave my life to the Lord and became a Christian for real. I was baptized. My God is real now in my life.

God has blessed me in so many ways since that day. My new wife is wonderful, Dad. She has been a Christian since she was nineteen years old. The children have become wonderful adults and are doing great. I could not count the blessings one by one, but there are many, many more.

Dad, you are in heaven, and I know I will join you someday. I try to love all people, and God has promised me eternal life by accepting Him as Lord and Savior. I love the Lord with all my heart. I ask you, Dad, to forgive me for the way I treated you. When I make it to heaven, I will not have to ask you to forgive me because you will already know.

Dad, I can't wait to see you in heaven. As Jim Hill said, "What a day that will be when my Jesus I shall see. And he takes me by the hand and leads me to the promised land." See you in heaven, Dad, where we will worship the Lord forever and ever. I love you forever, Dad.

Your youngest son, Duane

Whoever does not love does not know God, because God is love. (1 John 4:8 NIV)

So I say to you: Ask and it will be given to you; seek and you will find; knock and the door will be opened to you. (Luke 11:9 NIV)

If anyone, then, knows the good they ought to do and doesn't do it, it is sin for them. (James 4:17 NIV)

But God demonstrates his own love for us in this: While we were still sinners, Christ died for us. (Romans 5:8 NIV)

O God, you know my folly: my guilt is not hidden from you. (Psalm 69:5 NIV)

You will seek me and find me when you seek me with all your heart. (Jeremiah 29:13 NIV)

Ask, and it will be given to you. Seek and you will find. Knock, and the door will be opened to you. (Matthew 7:7 NIV)

I am so in love with Jesus that I would never bet again. This would hurt Him, and I wouldn't do anything to hurt Jesus. My life was full of misery and woe, but now my life is full of love. Oh, what a Savior! And now I know that I am going to heaven because God has promised me so. "Jesus, Jesus, Jesus! There is just something about that name!" Praise the Lord, his burden is light. He is everything for everybody. John 14.

In our house, we:

- Think positive
- Love one another

- Try to do better
- Say I am sorry
- Believe in grace
- Show respect
- Never give up
- Pray always

We try to work on these every day.
(Unknown)

Love: Mind over Matter

The hour I was saved, I told the Lord that I was sick and tired of being sick and tired. I wanted to make changes in my life—no more living like this. I've always said that I didn't grow up until I was forty-seven-years-old.

My motto is

- to be enthusiastic every day,
- to enjoy my life,
- to love my family,
- to love my neighbors,
- to love everyone I run into,
- to love my brothers and sisters,
- to help the poor, and
- to take the Bible to prisoners.

Your thoughts determine your attitude. God, keep that flag flying. God is love, God is wise, and God loves me. Come on, man. What is the problem?

I've heard people say, "I go to church because it makes me feel good." When I go to church, I go because I want to worship God and because I have the Holy Spirit within me. "Christ liveth in me. Christ liveth in me. O what a salvation this that Christ liveth in me" (Daniel W. Whittle 1891).

Once I died to my sin, I started living in eternity. I think of my wasted years. How foolish I was. He called through a life of wasted years. He touched me. Yes, He touched me. What joy. What peace. What love.

The question was asked: "Does everyone make it to heaven?" In heaven, everyone will worship and love Jesus. The answer to that is, "No. Because of sin, all won't make it to heaven. You must be born again. How you live down here on earth is how you will live in heaven."

Ten Ways to Love the Lord

1. Listen without interrupting. Proverbs 1:8
2. Speak without accusing. James 1:19
3. Give without sparing. Proverbs 21:26
4. Pray without ceasing. Colossians 1:9
5. Answer without arguing. Proverbs 17:1
6. Share without pretending. Ephesians 4:15
7. Enjoy without complaint. Philippians 2:14
8. Trust without wavering. 1 Corinthians 13:7
9. Forgive without punishing. Colossians 3:13
10. Promise without forgetting. Proverbs 13:12
(Unknown)

Praise, praise the Lord at all times!

Everyone thinks I'm crazy. They say, "You take this Jesus thing too seriously." Well, I don't know, but Christ took me pretty seriously when He died on the cross for me.

> Let no one seek his own, but each on the others' wellbeing. (1 Corinthians 10:24)

Those who walk with God always reach their destinations. God will take care of you. May everything I do be used to glorify You, my Lord.

> This is the day which the LORD hath made; we will rejoice and be glad in it. (Psalm 118:24 KJV)

> For the sake of his great name the LORD will not reject his people, because the LORD was pleased to make you his own. (1 Samuel 12:22 NIV)

Knowing God exists but choosing to remain lost is like knowing how to swim but choosing to drown.

> Let others see Jesus in me. (Ephesians 5:1)

When Jesus died on the cross, He was thinking of you and me. If you found out you were dying, would you be nicer, love more, or try something new? Well, you are, and we all are.

> He's all I need. I need not turn to any other for He's a friend, a friend who's closer than any brother. On this friend I can rely to be my strength as life goes by. He's the Lord of all and he's all I need. He's my everything. He is all I need. (Alvin Slaughter 1996)

Dear Lord, grant me the ability to speak kindly, to respond gently, and to hold my tongue at times. I want my actions and reactions to please and reflect You and Your love.

> Husbands, in the same way be considerate as you live with your wives, and treat them with respect

as the weaker partner and as heirs with you of the gracious gift of life, so that nothing will hinder your prayers. (1 Peter 3:7 NIV)

How Emotions Harm You

- Anger weakens the liver.
- Grief weakens the lungs.
- Worry weakens the stomach.
- Stress weakens the hearing and the brain.
- Fear weakens the kidneys.

(Unknown)

Money is numbers, and numbers never end. If it takes money to be happy, your search for happiness will never end. (Bob Marley)

- Good things come to those who believe.
- Better things come to those who are patient.
- And the best things come to those who don't give up.

(Unknown)

Let me be patient. Let me be kind. Make me unselfish without being blind. I may have faith to make mountains fall, but if I lack love, I am nothing at all. (Lauryn Hill)

God doesn't want us to have broken hearts, wounded emotions, and messed-up personalities. He wants us to know who we are in Christ and to receive His unconditional love.

Have you ever looked at your kids and had your heart filled with so much love and pride that it brought tears to your eyes? I have, and it is amazing. God is good!

It doesn't matter how big your house is, how recent your car is. Our graves will always be the same size. Stay humble. (Unknown)

You just can't give up on someone because the situation's not ideal. Great relationships aren't great because they have no problems. They are great because both people care enough about the other person to find a way to make it work.

Have I not commanded you to be strong and courageous? Do not be terrified. Do not be discouraged. For the Lord your God will be with you wherever you go. (Joshua 1:9 NIV)

Your past can never dictate your future when you put it in the hands of God. Amen.

Faith is taking the first step even when you don't see the whole staircase. Peace in the midst of the storm—priceless!

Treat people the way you want to be treated. Talk to people the way you want to be talked to. Respect is earned, not given. Sometimes the strongest among us are the ones who smile through silent pain, cry behind closed doors, and fight battles nobody knows about.

Having somewhere to go is a home. Having someone to love is a family. Having both is a blessing. (Unknown)

Sometimes you go through a mountain, and sometimes a sea. But God is always there. Amen.

Love

I chose goodness over evil that day. The day I was saved, Jesus came into my heart.

> Love is patient, love is kind. It does not envy, it does not boast, it is not proud. It does not dishonor others, it is not self-seeking, it is not easily angered, it keeps no record of wrongs. Love does not delight in evil but rejoices with the truth. It always protects, always trusts, always hopes, always perseveres. (1 Corinthians 13:4–8 NIV)

Love never fails. But where there are prophecies, they will cease; where there are tongues, they will be stilled; where there is knowledge, it will pass away.

There should be no talk of love in the Bible without sharing God's love for each of us. This is the love that has led to a path for eternal life. Praise God! God loves me; this I know, for the Bible tells me so.

To my children: When I tell you I love you, I don't say it out of habit or to make a conversation. I say it to remind you that you're the best thing that ever happened to me. You're truly a blessing.

Don't worry. God is never blind to your tears, never deaf to your prayers, and never silent to your pains. He sees, He hears, and He will deliver.

People have said to me that God didn't write the Bible; men did. Rest assured and know if God said it, that settles it.

Life has knocked me down a few times. It has shown me things I never wanted to see. I have experienced sadness and failures. But one thing is for sure: I always get up. I am a Christian. You can ridicule me. You can torture me. You can kill me. But you can't change my mind.

At the end, it isn't the years in your life that count. It is the life in your years. Weeping may endure for the night, but joy comes in the morning. Praise the Lord.

Lord, I ask you to protect my kids physically, emotionally, spiritually, mentally, and in every way.

> God is our refuge and strength. Always ready to
> help in times of trouble. (Psalm 46:1)

God has amazing things in your future. He has doors that will open wider than you thought possible. My mission is to try to help other gamblers to find Jesus Christ. He is the answer.

When I received Christ, I became a new person. As a new creation, Christ's love compels us to please God rather than ourselves. We look beyond the packaging of a person to what is inside. We have become altogether different people. We have been given a clean slate, a fresh start, and a new nature.

After twenty-three years as a Christian, to this day I still try to please God in everything I do. I try to let the Holy Spirit lead me. My life used to be all about me, about gambling. Now, I still like sports, but God comes first. Before, I would miss church and serve the devil instead of God. I do have a new start and a new nature.

I just watched the 700 Club. They interviewed two baseball players from the World Series. They said that being a baseball player is nice, but they gave God all the glory. They are saved, and that was the most important thing in their lives. When they die, they know they are not going to hell. They are going to heaven. Praise the Lord!

Family

I love my family so much, and I am proud of them. I think about how far we have come, and what wonderful blessings they are. To think that the way my life was before, I could have lost them. But by the grace of God, I have my wonderful family and my wife, and I am so proud of them. Yes, we have had a lot of ups and downs, but we are close now. She is my best friend. We are sensitive to one another's needs. We are living wonderful lives, and I know we will see each other in heaven when we die. Praise to the Lord! We will be together in eternity.

When my wife and I were dating, when we were together, it was like I was on top of the world. It was because I had a new life as a Christian, and I knew God had brought her to me.

> God's still working on me, and when I get to heaven God will say, "Well done." What a day that will be when my Jesus I shall see. (Jim Hill)

I saw on television the other day that these people get together and party, party, party. They said, "We just party. We don't talk about religion or politics. We just party." Well, they can do their thing; that is their business. But for me, I am going to serve the Lord, and when I get together with good Christian people, we talk about Jesus, Jesus, Jesus. When I get to heaven, I will have one big party with my Jesus and family. Amen.

I don't care what the headlines say. Because He lives, I can face tomorrow. Praise be to God. The love of God is far greater than tongue or pen can ever tell. It goes beyond the highest star and reaches to the lowest hell. The love of God is so rich and pure, so measureless and strong. It shall forevermore endure the saints' and angels' songs.

> The Lord bless you and keep you. The Lord make his face shine on you and be gracious to you; the Lord turn his face toward you and give you peace. Amen. (Numbers 6:24 NIV)

I look back on my life and wonder what my children felt. Did they feel loved when they didn't have a mother and had a dad who had a bad gambling problem? Did they not know which way to turn? Sometimes the people with the worst pasts end up creating the best futures.

Family Rules

1. Tell the truth.
2. Work hard.
3. Keep your promises.
4. Try new things.
5. Laugh out loud.
6. Use kind words.
7. Be grateful.
8. Be proud of yourself.
9. Remember that you are loved.

*   At my lowest, God is my hope.
*   At my darkest, God is my light.
*   At my weakest, God is my strength.
*   At my saddest, God is my comforter.
*   God is my everything.

(Unknown)

Thank you, Jesus.

*   When I fall, He lifts me up.
*   When I fail, He forgives.
*   When I am weak, He is strong.
*   When I face trials, he is with me.
*   When I am lost, he is the way.

Thank you, Jesus.

(Unknown)

As you waste your breath complaining about life, someone out there is breathing his or her last. Appreciate what you have. Be thankful and stop complaining. Live more, complain less, have more smiles, and less stress.

My greatest wish is that my children always know how much I love them, and that they walk through the rest of their lives knowing I'll always be there for them in any way I can.

Worry is a waste of time because it doesn't change anything. All it does is steal your joy and keep you very busy doing nothing.

Ten Things Money Can't Buy

1. Respect
2. Common sense
3. Integrity
4. Peace of mind
5. Patience
6. Happiness
7. Wisdom
8. Faith
9. Humility
10. Hope

Heavenly Father, You know every decision I need to make and every challenge I face. Please forgive me for the times that I try to figure this life out on my own. I need You. I need Your Holy Spirit to give me strength, wisdom, and direction. Nothing I have is because of luck or chance. It is all due to Your grace and favor. Amen.

Look at 1 Corinthians 10:23. A more literal translation of that verse is, "All things are permissible, but not all things promote growth in Christian character." The next time you question whether you should see a certain movie, participate in a specific activity, or engage in a certain habit, ask yourself the following questions.

1. Will the activity make the things of this world more appealing than the things of God?
2. Will it keep me from prayer?
3. Will it diminish my hunger for God's Word?
4. Will it spiritually tear me down by pulling me away from other Christian believers?

What a day that will be when my Jesus I shall see. (Jim Hill)

What is heaven going to be like? We will worship the King of all kings. I have property up there. We all will be together with loved ones. I have joy coming in the morning. God's still working on me, and He will say, "Well done, my good and faithful servant."

> Yet true godliness with contentment is itself great wealth. After all, we brought nothing with us when we came into the world, and we can't take anything with us when we leave it. So if we have enough food and clothing, a roof over our heads, let us be content. (1 Timothy 6:6)

But people who long to be rich fall into temptation and are trapped by many foolish, harmful desires that end in ruin and distraction. The love of money is the root of all kinds of evil. Some people, craving money, have wandered from the true faith and pierced themselves with many sorrows.

He was there all the time. One month after I became a Christian, I read in the paper that the bookie I was going to had shot someone in the bar where I had previously made my bets. It was a very small room. I think back on that, and it could have been me in that room, in the middle of that. He was there all the time. God is good all the time.

When I think of what God has done for me, I cry daily and wipe the tears away. I think about how much Jesus loves me; this I know, because the Bible tells me so.

Hope of the Future

For the evildoer has no future hope, and the lamp of the wicked will be snuffed out. (Proverbs 24:20 NIV)

Know also that wisdom is like honey for you: If you find it, there is a future hope for you, and your hope will not be cut off. (Proverbs 24:14 NIV)

> "For I know the plans I have for you," declares the Lord. "Plans to prosper you and not to harm you, plans to give you hope and a future." (Jeremiah 29:11 NIV)

Blessings When I Wasn't a Christian

In 1976, I had a lymph node operation. After the operation, the doctor told me it was cancer, and they were going to send my samples to John Hopkins Hospital to make sure. My parents and the church prayed for me for several days. My wife had me signed up in the cancer society. Five weeks later, the report came back that it was not cancer. Praise the Lord! God is good!

He was there all the time. God knows everything about us—more than we know about ourselves. God knows our futures. He knows when we will accept Him, like He knew that I would. He took care of me all through my teenage life and when I had an operation on my left eye in the eighth grade. When I was in the hospital at forty years old, my enzymes were up, and I was sent to intensive care. The nurses were trying to give me intravenous in my arms. They tried about five times, and I passed out. For seven seconds, my heart stopped. They worked on me, and I came to. Then I was sent to Pittsburgh for a heart cath. The doctor came into my room and told me my heart was fine. I asked the doctor what had happened back home. He said, "I think they almost scared you to death." He took out my pacemaker, and I was fine. God was truly with me.

People with understanding control their anger. A hot temper shows great foolishness. A perfect heart leads to a healthy body. Jealousy is like cancer in the bones.

> Turn my heart toward your statutes and not toward selfish gain. (Psalm 119:36 NIV)

God spoke to me the other night while listening to a sermon. He said, "Don't try to be like that person or another person. Just be yourself."

I bet on football, baseball, basketball, poker, horse racing, and dog racing for thirty years. But I have not bet on anything for twenty-three years since, not even a lottery ticket. God is good all the time. I love the Lord so much and do not want to hurt Him. When He saw that I meant business, He blessed me over and over again.

I feel called by God to share my experience about what gambling did to me and my family, and what it can do to others.

> I have fought the good fight. I have finished the race. I have kept the faith. Now there is in store for me the crown of righteousness which the Lord, the righteous judge, will award to me on that day. And not only to me, but also to all who have longed for his appearing. (2 Timothy 4:7–8 NIV)

Lord, help me understand that sports are nice to watch. But when I get to heaven, God is not going to say, "How are your Steelers doing?" That is why I need to slowly get away from these sports and think more of God and more of loving people. I hope these pro football players will think more of the Lord and others, and play football instead of trying to kill each other. Amen.

If We Don't Have a Vision

> Elijah had seen incredible works accomplished. (1 Kings 17:1, 12, 22; 18:19, 45)
>
> Fear will squash vision. (1 Kings 19:1–3; Matthew 25:25–26)
>
> The Word of the Lord comes to us. (Matthew 4:4; Jeremiah 23:29)
>
> When our vision is all about us, we can't see God's vision. (Genesis 4:9; Matthew 17:4)
>
> Vision can come to us any way God wants it to come. (Numbers 22:28; Job 38:1; 1 Samuel 3:10)
>
> Vision can come gently. (Psalm 46:10; John 8:11)

When we see God's vision, it lets us know we are not alone (Genesis 2:18). When I had a vision to write this book, I thought it was my vision. But I know now that it was God's vision for my life.

> If we meet and you forget me, you have lost nothing. But if you meet Jesus Christ and forget him, you have lost everything. (Dobson)

Why would anybody give up eternal life for money? All the money in the world is God's. We need to be good stewards of His money. The love of money is the root of all evil. You can't take it with you. It is well to have a good reputation in your life.

Home should be a sanctuary of love. Time with your family is a gift from God. God has given me the strength to bear my pain. Praise the Lord. Remember: no one is a failure as long as he or she has friends. Amen.

My hope is built on the solid rock. When I was into that gambling for thirty years, there was a void inside of me. What I went through happened; who I was existed. I needed my past and my mistakes to get me to where I am now.

I still believe in amazing grace, that there's power in the blood, that He walks with me and talks with me, and that because He lives, I can face tomorrow. All of this because of the old, rugged cross.

God is love. It's not over till the trumpet sounds (1 Peter 6–11).

Can you imagine being led by the Master's hand, His hand holding yours?

Dear Lord, thank you for giving me your strength so that I have the courage to move on. Your love, so that I can share it with others. Your wisdom, so that I can share your truth. Your mercy, so that I can forgive my enemies. Your peace, so that I can be still during the storms of life. Your hope, so that I won't quit and will never give up. Your joy, so that I'll be forever grateful for all You've done. Your grace, so that I am forgiven and healed, and my soul restored. Amen.

Life without Christ isn't really life at all. Christ liveth in me. Oh, how I love Jesus.

People were created to be loved. Things were created to be

used. The reason why the world is in chaos is because things are being loved and people are being used.

We Need Jesus

These are the most prevalent and destructive lies told today.

Lie #1: I am a good person. I do more good than bad.

The reality is that we have sinned and fall short of the glory of God. We need Jesus, and the world is being told it's okay without Him (Romans 6:23).

Lie #2: A loving God won't send anyone to hell.

God is a loving but just God. There has to be punishment for sin. We can choose Jesus's sacrifice or ultimately choose eternal separation from God in hell. The entire Bible teaches clearly that our relationship with God is the most important thing.

The cross gives you and me life. Through Christ's death on the cross, those who turn to Him are delivered from the penalty of sin. We must turn to Christ. The cross says that God especially loves those who are hurting and those who are under the penalty of sin. If you will turn to Jesus Christ and put your trust in what He did for you in taking your just penalty for sin on the cross, He will deliver you from sin's penalty and from its penalty and power. He wants to be your shepherd and overseer. He loves you just as you are, but He loves you too much to leave you that way. He wants to heal you from the devastating effects of sin. Will you turn to Him? I hope so. I have, and by doing so, I turned around my life.

Wasted Years

Have you lived without love? A life of tears? Have you searched for life's hidden meaning? Or is your life filled with long and wasted years? Wasted years—oh how foolish. (Jimmy Swaggart)

At the cross, at the cross, where I first saw the light, and the burden of my heart rolled away. It was there by faith I received my sight, and now I am happy all the day. (Isaac Watts 1707)

Glory to His name, there to my heart was the blood applied. Glory to His name. (Elisha A. Hoffman 1878)

So I'll cherish the old rugged cross till my trophies at last I lay down. I will cling to the old rugged cross. And exchange it some day for a crown. (George Bennard 1913)

The blessing of the LORD brings wealth, without painful toil for it. (Proverbs 10:22 NIV)

Blessed beyond measure—that's my wife and I. We're blessed in so many ways. Believe all things are possible. The old, rugged cross made the difference. I believe I have found my purpose in life: To love Jesus with all my heart, soul, body, and mind. To love my neighbor as myself. What a precious friend is Jesus.

What is Love?

Love is loving God because He first loved me. It is loving others because that's what God tells me to do. Love unconditionally. Love is patient. Love is kind.

Judas couldn't walk away from his silver, and so he lost his soul. People are losing their souls because of their gambling problems.

Choose to Live in Joy

Life goes by in the blink of an eye. It's too short to live upset, angry, resentful, or ungrateful. If you look for the good, you'll find it. Choose to be happy, to be at peace. Decide that each day is going to be a great day; grab each moment and make the best of it. Refuse to let negative thoughts take root in your mind. Refuse to let negative people and situations drag you down. Trust your journey and know that if you make a mistake, it's okay. See it as a lesson learned and keep moving forward.

> Spend less time worrying and more time being grateful for those who love you, and for all of God's goodness. Choose to live in joy. (Charity M. Richy Bently)

Have you ever looked back at your past and realized it was God who kept you alive? God kept me from going to prison. God kept me from getting shot. God must have known that I would accept Him as Lord and Savior.

There Is Joy in the Lord

> I have told you this so that my joy may be in you, and that your joy may be complete. (John 15:11 NIV)

There is joy in the Lord, there is joy in the Lord. Hallelujah, glory, glory. There is joy in the Lord. There is joy in the Lord.

What I Was Getting for My Money When I Gambled

When I gambled, I wasn't getting anything but

- trouble,
- heartache,

- less of loving my family and friends,
- less of loving my God,
- less money to help my family,
- less of paying my bills, and
- less of being friendly.

What wasted years!

Acts 11:24 (NIV) says, "Barnabas was a good man." But I think if you could talk to some of the people of Antioch, they would tell you he was one of the friendliest guys with whom they came in contact. Thank you, God, for all the friendly people in the world and for what they give to me when I am a stranger.

God made me to be uncomplicated in my faith, to watch children, kites, sunsets, and rainbows and enjoy them. He'll take your hand regardless of who you are or how you look. He'll accept you right where you are and love you unconditionally. Amen.

It is time to focus on how to love deeper and bring blessings and value to others in each moment we have here together.

If we live, we live for the Lord; and if we die, we die for the Lord. So, whether we live or die, we belong to the Lord. (Romans 14:8 NIV)

> However, as it is written: "What no eye has seen, what no ear has heard, and what no human mind has conceived" the things God has prepared for those who love him. (1 Corinthians 2:9 NIV)

The older I get, the quieter I become. Life humbles you so deeply as you age. You realize how much nonsense you've waste time on.

Choose life (Deuteronomy 30:19). That is what I did. I chose life over darkness, light over darkness. From now on, I am not looking back. Praise God! The day I accepted Jesus was the day my life changed forever. No more darkness.

JOY

J—Joy
O—Others
Y—Yourself

Look forward. Don't look back. Yesterday is history. Tomorrow is a mystery. Today is a gift.

Freedom in Christ

God clearly calls us to give up this cumbersome, defeating old self. I don't have to be a slave to sin to myself or to others in order to feel good about what I am. I don't have to have the world tell me what will make me happy. True freedom is realizing that apart from Christ, I am not free. If I want to experience this addictive aliveness, then I will throw off everything that hinders me from being truly alive.

The Writings of Reverend Russell Clarke

This was written by my dad, who since has gone to heaven and is living with the Lord. Dad died on March 4, 1992.

1

About Creation—About the Triune God!

> In the beginning God created the heavens and the earth. (Genesis 1:1 NIV)

> The heavens declare the glory of God; and the firmament showeth His handiwork. (Psalm 19:1; Romans 1:18–20 KJV)

Nature and humankind's conscience teach that God exists. The Bible does not try to prove that God exists. It shows God does indeed exist in many and varied ways.

> God who at sundry times and in divers manners spoke in the time past unto the fathers by the prophets, hath in these last days spoken unto us by His Son, whom he hath appointed heir of all things, by whom also he made the worlds. (Hebrews 1:1–2 KJV)

Christ was a part of the Godhead from the beginning of time. In Genesis 1:26, we see that Christ was involved in the creation of humankind. In 2 Corinthians 13:14 (KJV), we read, "The grace of the Lord Jesus Christ, and the love of God, and the communion of the Holy Ghost, be with you all. Amen." The Bible definitely teaches that the triune God is complete and factual in the term Father, Son, and Holy Spirit. The Holy Spirit gave orders to Christ's disciples, which indicates that he was part of the triune Godhead!

> While they were worshiping the Lord and fasting, the Holy Spirit said, "Set apart for me Barnabas and Saul for the work to which I have called them." (Acts 13:2 NIV)

We must have faith in God to experience His reality. In Hebrews 11:6 (NIV), we read, "But without faith it is impossible to please him; for he that cometh to God must believe that he is, and that God is a rewarder of them that diligently seek him." It should not be difficult for us to believe the miracle of creation, as recorded in the book of Genesis, when we read of Christ's miracles in the New Testament.

We have a definite statement, as recorded in Hebrews 11:3, that speaks of the miracle of creation. It speaks of things that God created were not made of things that could be seen. Please be careful to read this scripture verse.

> The disciples were given a definite promise by our Savior that he would not leave them alone after he left this world. He would come to them in the person of the Holy Spirit. (John 14:15–8)

A grandmother was taking a walk with her grandson one day, and as they walked, he said, "Grandma, I cannot understand this idea of the trinity." (God being one God, and still there are three persons in the trinity.) She was at a loss to explain it to him, and as she mulled it over in her mind, the boy exclaimed, "Oh! Grandma, I know how it is. There is the egg—the shell, the yolk, and the white—and still it is called an egg."

> If we will listen to God's Word as we read it, allowing the Holy Spirit to help us to understand it, he will use some very simple things to reveal God's truth to us. (1 Corinthians 1:26–28)

I was reading in a newspaper about a young woman who does blacksmith work and enjoys riding horses. She loves nature and God's wonderful out-of-doors. She had this to say about God. "To those who do not believe in God, no explanation would do. Those who believe in God need no explanation."

What Does the Bible Say Concerning Each Member or Person of the Trinity?

About God

The Bible says that God is unchangeable. "Every good gift and every perfect gift is from above, and cometh down from the Father of lights, with whom is no variableness, neither shadow of turning" (James 1:17 KJV).

God is eternal!

> Before the mountains were brought forth, or even thou hadst formed the earth and the world, even from everlasting to everlasting, thou art God. (Psalm 90:2 NIV)

God is almighty!

I am the almighty God! (Genesis 17:1 NIV)

God is everywhere!

Am I a God at hand, saith the Lord, and not far off? (Jeremiah 23:23 KJV)

God is omnipresent!

Can any hide himself in secret places that I shall not see him? Saith the Lord. Do not I fill Heaven and earth? Saith the Lord. (Jeremiah 23:23–24 KJV)

God is all-knowing!

Neither is there any creature that is not manifest in his sight; but all things are naked and open unto the eyes of Him with whom we have to do. (Hebrews 4:13 KJV)

God is holy!

Holy and reverend is His name. (Psalm 111:9 KJV)

Be ye holy, for I am holy. (1 Peter 1:16 KJV)

God is just!

And there is no God apart from me, a righteous God and a Savior; there is none but me. (Isaiah 45:21 NIV)

God is love!

> He that loveth not, knoweth not God; for God is love. (1 John 4:8 KJV)

God is a God of mercy!

> The Lord, the Lord God, merciful and gracious, long suffering, and abundant in goodness, and truth, keeping mercy for thousands, forgiving iniquity and transgressions and sin. (Exodus 34:6–7 KJV)

God is a God of truth!

> It was impossible for God to lie. (Hebrews 6:18 KJV)

About Christ

Christ is called God!

> In the beginning was the Word, and the Word was with God, and the Word was God. He was with God in the beginning. Through him all things were made; without him nothing was made that has been made. (John 1:1–3 NIV)

Note the words "through him all things were made." Of course, the word "him" refers to Christ.

Because Christ is called God, this tells us that Christ is eternal in existence. Even as God is spoken of as unchangeable, so Christ is spoken of in the same manner.

> Jesus Christ, the same yesterday, and today, and forever. (Hebrews 13:8 KJV)

Christ is also spoken of as everywhere present (Matthew 18:20).

Jesus is all-powerful!

> And Jesus came and spoke unto them, saying, all power is given unto me in heaven and in earth. Go ye therefore and teach all nations … and lo, I am with you always, even unto the end of the world. Amen. (Matthew 28:18–20 KJV)

Christ is all-knowing!

> Lord thou knowest all things: thou knowest that I love Thee. (John 21:17 KJV)

Jesus was worshiped even as God (John 5:23; 1 Corinthians 1:2).

About the Holy Spirit

The Holy Spirit is also called the Holy Ghost. He is spoken of as a person (John 16:13–14).

The Holy Spirit operated in the creation of the world (Genesis 1:2).

The writing of the scriptures is spoken of as being inspired of God (2 Timothy 3:16). The Holy Spirit, the third person of the trinity, had a definite part in moving upon the hearts of holy men to speak God's Word (2 Peter 1:21).

The Crowning Work of Creation: Humankind!

> So God created man in his own image, in the image of God created He him: male and female created He them. (Genesis 1:27 KJV)

God was holy, and so He created humans as holy beings.

The story of humankind's fall from a holy state to a sinful state is told in the third chapter of Genesis. Humans fell from a holy state to a lower nature, a sinful nature.

God's instruction given to humans to not partake of the fruit of a tree in the middle of the garden of Eden indicates that God gave humans the power of choice. In other words, God made humans free moral agents. And when Adam and his wife chose to disobey God, the curse of sin came into their lives. The nature of sin, the inbred sin, became a part of humankind's nature (Genesis 3:2–3; 17:22, 24).

We see the penalty pronounced on humankind for their disobedience. Adam Clark has this to say concerning Genesis 3:15: "The serpent that tempted Adam and Eve was actuated by the Devil, that we are not to look for merely literal meaning here: that God in his endless mercy has put enmity between men and Satan."

We see that according to Genesis 3:15, the seed here spoken of is a promise of the fact that Christ, the only Son of God, would one day come into the world, be born of the virgin Mary, and suffer and die on the cross of Calvary to purchase humankind's salvation. When humans fell from their high state of moral purity to a low state of sin and degradation, God had definite plans for their redemption.

We read in Acts 26:18 (NIV) these words: "to open their eyes and turn them from darkness to light, and from the power of Satan to God, so that they may receive forgiveness of sins and a place among those who are sanctified by faith in me."

Regarding the fall of humankind into a low sinful state, although the consequences were terrible not only for Adam and Eve but for the whole human race, God was merciful and provided a deliverer, Jesus Christ!

2

Sin

Now, let us take a look at sin and its terrible blight upon the lives of human beings. We notice these words of King David as recorded in Psalm 51:5 (KJV). "Behold I was shapen in iniquity; and in sin did my Mother conceive me." This tells us that since the fall of Adam and Eve into sin, and as sin entered into their nature, their posterity reaps the results of that fall. They had that nature passed on to them.

Humans have the natural inclination to sin as soon as they come to the age of accountability. Some come to a sense of awareness of wrongdoing earlier than others. In Romans 3:23 (KJV) we read, "For all have sinned and come short of the glory of God."

According to Genesis 2:17, sin in its original sense is a want of obedience to divine law, and that still is the case. When Adam and Eve disobeyed God, doing what He told them not to do, they died in a spiritual sense. They were alienated or separated from God. They lost fellowship with God. They lost God's favor. Their hearts were no longer in tune with God. They lost their formed, happy relationship with God, and of this they were very conscious.

In the book of Ephesians, I am going to copy from the Revised Standard Version of the Bible the scripture verses so as to show the reader what takes place when a sinner is brought back into a proper relationship with God.

> And you He made alive, when you were dead through the trespasses and sins in which you once walked, following the prince of the power of the air, the spirit that is now at work in the sins of disobedience. Among these we all once lived in the passions of our flesh, following the desires of body and mind, and so we were by nature children of wrath, like the rest of mankind. But God, who is rich in mercy, out of the great love with which he loved us, even when we were dead through our trespasses, made us alive together with Christ (by grace you have been saved) and raised us up with Him, and made us sit with Him in the heavenly places in Christ Jesus, that in the coming ages he might show the immeasurable riches of his grace in kindness toward us in Christ Jesus.
>
> For by grace you have been saved through faith, and this is not your doing, it is the gift of God— not because of works, lest any man should boast. For we are His workmanship created in Christ Jesus for good works, which God prepared beforehand, that we should walk in them. (Ephesians 2:1–10 RSV)

The Holy Spirit convicts the sinner and makes him or her very conscious of the sinfulness of the committed sins, wooing the sinner to repent and be converted (John 16:8–11; John 6:44).

In our time right now, sin is ruining the lives of untold millions. Men and women are committing terrible crimes and sins. There is so much moral corruption, so much greed and dishonesty. And who knows what is going on in the dark recesses of the sinful pattern of life? Jesus Christ is the only answer for a sinful world.

Still some would tell us that the way to live is to do what you want to do, whatever you feel comfortable with. The comfortable thing with them is to live immoral lives, to live with the opposite sex without the benefit of a proper marriage, to smoke pot, and to do other things freely and readily regardless of what God's Word has to say. But, dear sinner friend, remember the words of the wise man as written in Ecclesiastes 12:13–14 (KJV).

Let us hear the conclusion of the whole matter: fear God and keep His commandments, for this is the whole duty of humankind. For God shall bring every work into judgment, with every secret thing, whether it be good or whether it be evil. If some choose to not believe God's Bible while they live in this world, it will be too late for them to believe and repent after they leave this world.

God has appointed a day in which he will judge the world (Acts 17:31).

The Plan of Salvation

We have seen how God planned for humankind's redemption right at the time humans fell from the lofty state of holiness to a low state of sin, reaping some of the consequences right here in this world. This plan for the redemption of humankind was to be brought about by God's Son Jesus Christ coming into this world to die for humankind's redemption. This great truth is summed up in what we call the Golden Text of the Bible: "For God so loved the world that He gave His only begotten Son, that whosever believeth in Him might not perish but have everlasting life" (John 3:16 KJV).

For a while in the history of humankind, God established a system of animal sacrifices. This was instituted in the system of laws that God gave to Moses. These animal sacrifices prefigured the sacrifice Christ would offer by dying on the cross for our salvation.

Humans fell into a state of spiritual death and a continued pattern to sin, and we see how God planned for their restoration to a right and proper relationship with God, our heavenly Father. Christ gives life and immortality to every soul who believes in Him and trusts in His plan of salvation.

We read in 1 Peter 19:20 (KJV) how this is brought about. "But with the precious blood of Christ, as of a lamb without blemish and without spot; who verily was foreordained before the foundation of the world, but was manifested in these last times for you."

It has been said by more than one individual that if they had been the only sinners in the world, they believe Jesus would have come into this world and died for them. And He would have.

Jesus said in John 14:6 (NIV), "I am the way and the truth and the life." It is through Christ that we may be raised from an old life of sin and rebellion against God to walk in newness of life in Christ.

In 2 Corinthians 5:17 (KJV), we read, "Therefore if any man be in Christ he is a new creature; old things are passed away, behold, all things are become new."

Remember that sin places humans in a state of death. Read Ephesians 2:1. (Note "dead in trespasses and in sin.") It is from this state that Christ raises us to a total new life in Him.

What Must I Do to Be Saved?

Paul and Silas told the Philippian jailer, "Believe on the Lord Jesus Christ, and thou shalt be saved" (Acts 16:31 KJV). Faith is not to be confused with mere acknowledgment of a historical Christ. Hear these words from James 2:19: "Thou believest that there is one God; thou doest well; the devils also believe and tremble. But wilt thou know, O vain man, that faith without works is dead?" Believing in Christ for our souls' salvation means accepting His teaching, His way of life, and living by His principles.

We are not saved by going through a set ritualistic pattern or by doing good works. We are saved through genuine repentance, turning away from our old, sinful patterns to walk in a new life with Christ. After we have acknowledged our sinful lives, repented of our sins, and asked God for Christ's sake to forgive us, then by faith we accept His salvation. Good works follow in the life of the Christian after he is saved by faith in our Lord Jesus Christ.

Ephesians 2:8–13 explains in very vivid language just what takes place as we become Christians. There are different biblical terms that explain the experience of becoming a Christian.

The New Birth

Read the Gospel of John 3:1–8. What did Christ mean when he told Nicodemus that he must be born again? Our Lord was telling Nicodemus that it was not a physical rebirth, but a new birth, a new creation in the souls of humans. Perhaps a lot of people wish they could be physically reborn and start life over. But the miracle that Jesus was talking about was this: that by His divine power, one can begin a new beginning by being recreated in Christ's divine image.

Being Saved

I have already dealt briefly with this subject, but I would like to further state that being saved means that after the sinner repents and forsakes his or her past life of sin and turns to Christ with all his or her heart, the sinner passes from the state of spiritual death to a new life in Christ.

The sinner is saved from a past life of sin and sinful practices, and from the terrible consequences of sin. He or she is given the hope of eternal life in Christ, through faith in His promise that whoever comes to Him in true repentance, He will not cast out (John 6:37).

Regeneration

In Titus 3:5–6 (NIV), we read, "Not by works of righteousness which we have done, but according to His mercy He saved us, by the washing of regeneration, and renewing of the Holy Ghost; which He shed on us abundantly through Jesus Christ our Savior." This regeneration process is part of the salvation experience as we become born-again Christians. This is a renewal experience.

In Romans 8:16 (KJV), we read, "The Spirit itself beareth witness with our spirit that we are all children of God." Our nature is changed from a way of life that is out of the will of God, to a way of life that is in the will of God. I will name one more term that the Bible speaks of that relates to the salvation experience.

Redemption

To be redeemed means that we are set free from the power and habits of sin through the shed blood of Christ, who is our Redeemer. We read in Romans 6:18 (KJV), "Being then made free from sin, ye became the servants of righteousness."

There are several terms or expressions in the Bible that are used to explain what the salvation experience is, but they all relate to the same general experience.

Sanctification

Sanctification is a Bible doctrine. It is an experience that follows our experience of conversion. Let us notice in Acts 26:18 (KJV) these words. "To open their eyes, and to turn them from darkness to light, and from the power of Satan unto God, that they may receive the forgiveness of sins, and inheritance among them which are sanctified by faith that is in me." This is Jesus talking in this verse of scripture. Now let us notice what He is saying. Jesus is telling the apostle Paul, at the time of his conversion, that he was to preach to the Gentiles (people other than Jews) and help them to understand the gospel, to open their eyes and understanding by the preaching of the gospel and their need of salvation from sin.

In this connection, we read in John 16:8–10 that it is one of the office works of the Holy Spirit to convince one of their need of a savior. Paul was to preach and show the Gentiles that as they repented of their sins and turned from sin to God through true and sincere repentance, God would forgive them. And it would be because the Holy Spirit would convince them that this would come about.

Going back now to Acts 26:18, Paul was to tell the Gentiles that subsequent to their conversion experience, they were to consecrate their saved lives to God and His service, and receive the baptism of the Holy Spirit.

This text speaks of two works of grace: being saved and sanctified.

Did you notice in this text these words? It speaks of the forgiveness of sins, and sins is a plural word. When sinners come to Christ for salvation, what are they thinking of? It is the burden of sins on their hearts that is weighing them down. They ask for forgiveness of these sins.

Remember, when Adam and Eve sinned, they passed the seed of sin on to the entire human race. Recall David saying, "In sin did my mother conceive me" (Psalm 51:5 KJV).

When sinners come to Christ at the outset of their conversion experience, they repents of their sins that they have committed. They are completely accountable for the sins that they have committed. They are not accountable for the nature of sin passed on to them by Adam (1 Corinthians 15:22).

As the converted sinners grow in grace, they come to understand that there is a need of a deeper work of grace for which they need to consecrate (Romans 12:1–2). We see that according to the gospel record, the disciples' names were written in heaven (Luke 10:20).

A little later on, they witnessed the death of Christ on the cross to pay their redemption price for their salvation. They were forgiven of their committed sins, but a deeper work of grace was needed in their hearts. Jesus said that the Spirit was with them, but He shall be in you (John 14:17). There were still signs of a carnal nature in their lives (Luke 9:54).

It seems not only from a biblical standpoint, but also from a practical and logical view, that we are to dedicate a saved life to the service of God. The time for the seal of the Holy Spirit to be placed on our lives is at the time of our consecration of our saved lives to allow the Holy Spirit to come into our lives in complete surrender to His service (Ephesians 1:13).

The Purpose

Why and for what purpose do we consecrate our born-again lives for the infilling of the Holy Spirit? Let us see what the Master said about this. In Acts 1:8 (KJV), we read, "But ye shall receive power after the Holy Ghost is come upon you; and ye shall be witnesses unto me both in Jerusalem, and in all Judea, and in Samaria, and unto the uttermost part of the earth." We see here that the purpose of the Holy Spirit baptism was to empower Christ followers to live holy lives and give them the boldness that they would need to witness to the saving and keeping power of the blood of Christ.

A witness in this case is to tell others who need the saving grace of our Lord Jesus Christ what the Lord has done for us, and what He will do for them also if they will allow Him to come into their hearts and lives.

3

Bible Holiness

Holiness of life is a Bible doctrine. Even in Old Testament times, our Lord called for a certain degree of holiness. In Leviticus 19:2 (KJV), we read, "Ye shall be holy; for I the Lord your God am holy." reaching a certain degree of holiness of life observing moral and ethical principles, as they understood them. But we see from what the apostle Paul has to say about the weakness of the old Mosaic law and animal sacrifices, as recorded in Hebrews 10:1–14. (Note particularly the first, fourth, ninth, and tenth verses.) We are told in this chapter that the blood of bulls and goats could not take away sins. We see in Hebrews 10:16–17 that it was made possible for an individual to be made victorious over sin and sinful habits by the supreme sacrifice that Christ made in dying on the cross of Calvary.

Now let us note a few more texts that teach the doctrine of holiness. In Hebrew 12:14 we read, "Follow peace with all men, and holiness without which no man shall see the Lord." See also Peter 2:21–22. If we follow in Christ's footsteps (His example), we won't go very far astray. In fact, we are taught to follow His steps "who did no sin, neither was guile found in His mouth" (1 Peter 2:21–22).

The apostle Paul taught holiness of life (1 Corinthians 15:34). The apostle John taught the holiness of life (1 John 1:6–9). Some teach the eighth verse to mean that everybody does sin all the time, because it says, "If we say that we have no sin." But the apostle explains what he meant in the tenth verse (if we say that we have not sinned, etc.). John did teach holiness of life according to verses 6–7 of 1 John, as well as elsewhere in his epistles. Verses eight and ten of 1 John 1 is talking about people who say they didn't have any sin to be forgiven of.

We do read in the scripture that all have sinned and come short of the glory of God. Until the individual repents and forsakes a sinful life, he or she is a sinner who needs forgiveness of sins. After sinners come to know Christ in sincerity, then they are new creatures, and they are not bound any longer (unless they choose to go back into the life of sin); they are free people, made free from the old life to walk in a new life with Christ.

Sin is represented as being in darkness (1 John 1:6–7). When we are delivered from that darkness of sin, we now walk in the light of God's forgiveness.

The apostle Paul describes this new lifestyle very vividly in Ephesians 4:17–32. Also, the apostle Peter describes the lifestyle of a born-again Christian, a sanctified person (1 Peter 2:9–12). I would like very much if the reader would take the time to read the above scriptures, because they very vividly explain the truth that I have been trying to portray as distinctly and vividly as possible.

The Christian people are called the bride of Christ; He is called the bridegroom (John 3:29). The Christian is also spoken of as having partaken of the divine nature (2 Peter 1:4). These terms indicate a close relationship with Christ, the Son of God. Such a relationship calls for holiness of life in the individual Christian, as well the entire church of God, worldwide.

It has been said that our holiness of life is a relative holiness in our relationship to Christ. Perhaps this is true because of our humanity. But we must realize that the Bible does call for a definite type of holiness in this dispensation of the grace of God, as over against the Old Testament dispensation of laws, ritualism, etc. (Colossians 3:16–17).

Some Objections to Bible Holiness

Some scriptures that people use to try to prove that all sin, more or less (their true meaning). In 1 Kings 8:46 (KJV), we read, "If they sin against thee (for there is no man that sinneth not)." In Ecclesiastes 7:20 (KJV) we read, "For there is not a just man upon the earth, that doeth good, and sinneth not." These scriptures were uttered by Solomon about one thousand years before Jesus Christ came and made a perfect atonement for sin.

I have previously described the inferior power and ability of Old Testament animal sacrifices to take away sin. Christ's superior sacrifice in this day of grace made it possible for us to be delivered from sin; see again Hebrews 10:1–14. Humans can now live holy lives. (Titus 2:11–14).

Let us notice in Matthew 19:16–17 (KJV) these words: "And behold, one came and said unto Him, 'Jesus, Good Master, what good thing shall I do that I may have eternal life?' And He said unto him, 'Why callest thou me good? There is none good but one, that is God.'" No one possesses goodness without God's help. It is also possible that Christ wanted the Jews, as well as this young ruler, who asked, "What must I do to obtain eternal life?" to understand that He was indeed a part of the Godhead, that He was divine. It is said of Jesus that He did no sin (1 Peter 2:22).

Another scripture that people use to try to prove that it is impossible to live a holy life is found in Romans 3:10 (KJV). Here we see the phrase, "None righteous. No, not one." Note whom the apostle Paul is speaking of in this chapter. Please read verses 10–18. He was speaking of a wicked class of people. Note these phrases: none seek after God, none do good, they are deceitful, they curse, they shed blood, they do not have peace, no fear of God. These context verses following verse 10 teach us that we must pay close attention to the context when reading the Bible.

God's people are righteous people. In Titus 2:11–12 (KJV), we read, "For the grace of God that bringeth salvation hath appeared to all men, teaching us that, denying ungodliness, and worldly lust, we should live soberly, righteously, and godly in this present world." Note that word, *present*. You see, it is now (while we live) that we are to live righteous lives. We cannot build a theology on one verse of scripture. We must pay attention to the context.

4

Christian Growth

But grow in grace and in the knowledge of our
Lord and Savior Jesus Christ. (2 Peter 3:18 NIV)

After you become a Christian, begin to read God's Word
regularly, and develop a regular prayer life, you begin to grow
in the knowledge of God's Word. You may feel that when you
first become a Christian, you lack very much in being able to
understand God's Word. Do not become discouraged. In James
1:5 we read, "If any of you lack wisdom, let him ask of God." This
is natural for a new Christian. Be patient, but be persistent and
be faithful in Bible study, attending worship services in a solid,
Bible-believing church. Use good Bible study materials to help
you. I am convinced that what I have written in this book will
help you. I feel that God has directed me in this work. I have been
a Bible student for over sixty years. I write out of a pure heart and
clear and clean motives.

The Bible speaks of young Christians as babes in Christ. "As
newborn babes, desire the sincere milk of the word, that ye may
grow thereby" (1 Peter 2:2 KJV).

As you read and study God's Word, it will help you to remain a clean, pure Christian (Psalm 119:9).

Memorizing the Word of God as much as we can will help us to fight the good fight of faith and overcome temptation. In Psalm 119:11 (KJV) we read, "Thy word have I hid in mine heart, that I might not sin against thee."

Jesus is our best example to follow as Christians. I would recommend to Christians that they read in Matthew 4:1–11 how Jesus dealt with temptations, and that they follow His example. Notice these points to always remember.

1. Read the Bible.
2. Pray regularly.
3. Obey; see 1 Peter 1:14.
4. Witness; see Acts 1:8 and James 5:20.
5. Be assured of victory; see 1 Corinthians 10:13.

The New Testament Church

Christ established His church while here on earth (Matthew 16:18). This scripture does not mean that our Lord established His church on Peter, but on the confession, or element of truth, that Peter expressed. We read in God's Word that Christ is the head of His church (Colossians 1:18; Ephesians 2:19–22).

We see the importance of consulting other verses of scripture at this point to understand the nature of God's church. I have attempted to do so this to properly explain Matthew 16:18. We read in 1 Corinthians 12:12–20 that the church is made up of individuals. We also see that salvation (or becoming a born-again Christian) makes us members of His church (Acts 2:47).

Christians are represented in the Bible as sheep, and non-Christians are represented as goats (Matthew 25:32–46). We see in these verses that it will be Christians who will be received to enter the heaven that Christ has gone to prepare for them, and the non-Christians will not be privileged to enter heaven. God's people are a separate people, called out of the world of sin to walk in newness of life.

Only the saved or born-again Christians are members of God's church (Acts 20:28). The word *church* means "called-out ones." We know that many Christians have joined some individual church organizations, but this was not the case when Christ first built His church. It was, and still is, His will that all Christians be one body in Him (John 17:20–21). This is not to say that Christians scattered in various denominations are not members of God's church. Jesus did say in John 10:16 (KJV), "And other sheep I have, which are not of this fold; Them I also must bring, and they shall hear my voice. And there shall be one fold, and one Shepherd." Whether this will be fulfilled in this life, I do not know. But it could happen through persecution that God's people will be brought together.

This is a big subject. I suggest that the reader make further study of it.

Honoring Christ

In speaking of our redemption through Christ, I would like to emphasize the loftiness and honor that belong to Him alone. Some would have us believe that Christ was not the only begotten Son of God, that He was a good man among many good men, or a son among many sons of God. In Colossians 3:11 we read that Christ is "all in all" in His church.

No human being could use the words that Christ did, as shown in John 17:1–8. Please read these verses. We only have one Redeemer and that is Christ. No religious leader of a humanly organized religion is a redeemer. Only Christ is humankind's Redeemer. Only He paid the price for our redemption. The words spoken by the apostle Paul in Acts 2:32–33 can only be spoken of our Savior Jesus Christ.

Notice Philippians 2:8–11, where it speaks of Christ's death on the cross for our salvation (our redemption), and of God exalting and giving Him a name that is above every name. It states that every tongue shall confess that Jesus Christ is Lord, to the glory of God the Father.

There is no way that Jesus Christ should be put on a level with Buddha, Mohammed, or any other human religious leader of the past or present. He transcends them all in life and death, and in the fact that He arose from the grave and ever lives to intercede for all that will come to Him for salvation from sin.

5

The Gifts of the Spirit

I do not feel that I can overemphasize the importance of having a general knowledge of the Bible, as well as exercising care to observe the context of various scriptures (that is, the particular text we use in studying different subjects). In dealing with the gifts of the Spirit, the above rule will be well to follow. We should carefully consider the fruits of the Spirit first. One should be a truly born-again Christian and have committed his or her saved life completely to God, asking for and receiving the baptism of the Holy Spirit. The Bible tells us that our heavenly Father will give the Holy Spirit to them that ask (Luke 11:13). Jesus told His apostles that the Holy Spirit dwelt with them, and He shall be in you (John 14:17).

But from the time we become Christians we should begin to manifest the fruits of the Spirit. If we want a gift of the Spirit, we must first manifest the fruits of the Spirit. We are in no position to receive a gift of the Spirit if we do not manifest the fruits of the Spirit in our lives (Galatians 5:22–26). The apostle Paul tells us that the best way to represent our Lord is to manifest His love in our hearts and lives (1 Corinthians 12:3; 13:1–8).

Let's discuss the gifts of the Spirit. Let us notice in 1 Corinthians 12:8–11 what the gifts are; please also read Romans 12:5–8. To conserve space in these writings, I hope that you will read all scripture portions that I have mentioned. Notice that it is the Holy Spirit that gives gifts, and therefore they are supernaturally given. The Holy Spirit makes the choice of what gift to give and to whom it is to be given. One cannot have all the gifts (1 Corinthians 12:29–30). We do not pick out a gift, whether it is speaking in tongues, preaching, or whatever (1 Corinthians 12:11).

It is true that the Holy Spirit may give us a gift that has some relationship to some of our natural abilities (1 Timothy 4; Matthew 23:15).

We see that according to the twelfth and fourteenth chapters of 1 Corinthians, the gifts are given for the profit of all the family of God. They are not given just for personal enjoyment. In 1 Corinthians 12:13–31, we see the value of all the gifts to the entire body, or church of God. It even mentions "helps." I once read about a lady in Akron, Ohio, who would leave home early on Sunday evening to go to church. Her purpose was to stop at the home of a lady who was sick and tidy up her home for her. There are men who have worked long hours for the church, doing some repair work. I would say that these are some of the works that come under the heading of the gifts of "helps." See also Romans 16:3.

The apostle Paul compares the church to the human body. The body is composed of different members, and each member has its own distinct function, but even so the church is composed of different members, and each individual has his or her own particular gift and place in the church. In this we see the value of each individual gift for the edification, or value, to the entire body of Christ, or church of God.

I do not wish to make a lengthy study of all the gifts, but permit me to say something concerning the gifts of knowledge and wisdom. The best way to explain these gifts is to let the Bible speak to us as to the kind of wisdom and knowledge that is spoken of and therefore given to certain individuals: special gifts to open up some of the deep mysteries of the message of the gospel (Colossians 2:2–9). Matthew 23:34 may refer to the gifts of wisdom and knowledge. Certainly the apostles Peter and Paul were given wisdom to resolve problems that arose in the early church (Acts 15:1–19).

The Gift of Tongues

Please read carefully Acts 2:1–18. Notice these facts.

There were, according to Acts 1:15, about 120 apostles and others present on the day of Pentecost. The Lord had told them to wait for the promise of the Father—namely, to be baptized with the Holy Spirit. No doubt in those ten days of waiting, they had consecrated their saved lives to the service of the Master. They were told that they would receive power. Power for what? To live in and walk with the Spirit (Galatians 5:16). Also, they would receive power to witness for Christ, to live righteous lives, and to be good examples of the Christlike life.

There were gathered together at this time in Jerusalem people "of every nation under Heaven." When they heard the apostles and other Christians speak in their language, they were amazed. We see here that the word *unknown*, as used in the King James Version of the scriptures, really meant that it was a language; see verse eight.

Speaking in a foreign language by the disciples was not for the purpose to witness to the disciples that they had received the baptism of the Holy Spirit. It was for the purpose of the people gathered together from various nations to hear the gospel in their own language.

The Holy Spirit does not use miraculous happenings to indicate His own presence in the heart of the believer. He is His own witness (Romans 8:16; Acts 15:8–9). There is no indication in the New Testament that one has to speak in a different language as evidence that one has the baptism of the Holy Spirit.

If one used Mark 16:17–18 to try to prove that people should speak in a tongue other than their native tongues in order to prove that they have received the baptism of the Holy Spirit, then could it not also be said that if they cast out a devil, picked up a serpent, or drank a deadly poison, these events would also prove they had received the Holy Spirit? Remember that we receive the baptism of the Holy Spirit by faith (Acts 15:9). We receive the second work of grace in the same way we receive the original conversion experience.

We note that after the day of Pentecost, on various occasions some spoke in foreign languages, and at other times they did not. Note that in Acts 10:44–47, the Gentiles did speak in a foreign language. There must have been a need for this, or they would not have spoken thus. There was a need and a reason for the disciples to speak in a foreign language on the day of Pentecost. The same can be said of the twelve at Ephesus (Acts 19:1–6). The apostle Paul did not speak in tongues (Acts 9:17–18; 8:14–17). Here, Peter and John went down to Samaria after they had heard of some of the Samaritans becoming Christians, and they prayed for them that they might receive the Holy Spirit (or be sanctified), and these people by faith received the Holy Spirit. They did not speak in a foreign language.

Now, let us go to chapter 14 of 1 Corinthians. At the outset, remember that all gifts had a definite purpose, and they were given for the benefit of all the church, or congregation of believers, and to enlighten the unbelievers to understand the things of God. But in the matter of speaking in tongues, it would all depend on the need to speak in another language in order that the listeners may receive spiritual enlightenment. You will understand this better as I proceed.

Before we go into the fourteenth chapter of 1 Corinthians, let us think back and take note of what happened on the day of Pentecost. There were people present from all nations (Acts 2:8–11). They were able to hear the gospel in their own tongues. We see in 1 Corinthians 14 that the apostle Paul is also saying that to speak in a foreign language (the gift of speaking in a foreign tongue) was for the purpose of enlightenment. He says that if no one present can understand what is being said, it is like talking into the air (verse 9).

It will also be seen in verses 27–28 that if a person has the gift of tongues or can speak in another language other than his or her own tongue, this person also has the ability to control him- or herself, so as not to use that language unless it is absolutely necessary.

Sleep Benefit

What about an individual being by themselves, or if in a public meeting with others? Should you pray (or exhort), using a foreign tongue, or should you pray or speak for the benefit of others in your native tongue?

Let us notice 1 Corinthians 14:2–4 and 13–14. It would seem that some in the Corinthian church got off on the wrong track in regard to what the purpose of using a foreign language was for. Paul seems to be telling them in these few verses that even in private prayer, it would be better to use your own native tongue rather than to speak or think in terms of a foreign language. If you do use another language, pray that you may be able to interpret it.

You may feel good about it in spirit, even if you do use a foreign language, but your understanding will be unfruitful. I personally have been praying or meditating and felt very much lifted in spirit, but I only thought in relation to my native tongue, English.

Most Important

Of all the gifts that the apostle Paul mentions in 1 Corinthians 12:28–31, he places speaking of tongues as the least importance. He does make some exception, providing the one who speaks interprets what he says. And of course, it goes right back to the fact that there should be a need to use a foreign language.

So we find that Paul places more importance on preaching and Holy Spirit–led exhortations than the gift of speaking in a foreign language. Paul also emphatically states that all do not speak or have the gift of tongues (1 Corinthians 12:30e). Remember that Paul told Timothy to rightly divide the word of truth.

In a further discussion of the subject in 1 Corinthians 14, we receive more light on the subject. We need to study this chapter in its relationship to the second chapter of Acts, and indeed with respect to all he says in chapters 12–14 of 1 Corinthians. By doing so, we come up with facts and a lot less confusion. I am seventy-nine years old; I know what confusion the tongues movement caused back in the twenties and thirties. I was just a young man. In the church I attended, there was a man who had a clear-cut testimony of a good Christian experience, but he took up with the tongue movement. Later on, he told me he would have been better off staying with the church of God. He not only was confused with that teaching, but he was beginning to lean toward a cult's teaching.

I do not mean to say that all who speak in tongues are not Christians. I do believe that I have given a frank and sound interpretation of scripture. I have written very frankly about the gift of speaking in another tongue.

In closing this section, some believe that all Christians should speak with another tongue, and unless they do, they do not have the Holy Spirit. I simply am saying that I believe many people misinterpret the Bible. I feel that I have given good reasons for my belief.

Healing and the Gift of Healing

Let us note first of all that the Bible teaches that God does indeed heal sick bodies. He has healed, and He will heal. We read in Hebrews 13:8 that Jesus Christ is the same yesterday, today, and forever. In Isaiah 53:45, we see the prophecy that the Messiah would heal the sick when He came into the world. In Matthew 8:16–17, we read about the fulfillment of the prophecy. Jesus did heal to show that He had the power to heal (Matthew 9:5–7). He has power not only to forgive sins, but also to heal the body. But Jesus also healed out of a heart of compassion (Matthew 20:34). In the commission that Christ gave His apostles before leaving this world, a part of the blessing that would follow the preaching of the gospel was, "They shall lay hands on the sick and they shall recover." We believe in the gospel through the written Word of God. The promise as given in Matthew 21:22 is for us today. Of course, if we do not believe, then the promises as given in God's Word are not for us.

If we believe in creation as we read about in the book of Genesis, it should not be difficult to believe in God's promise for us today. He brought about creation by His spoken Word. We read in 2 Corinthians 1:20 (KJV), "For all the promises of God in Him (Christ) are yea, and in Him Amen, unto the glory of God by us."

In my home before I was married, healings were experienced.

In our own home, my wife and I have experienced healings, as have our children. My wife was healed of facial paralysis. The church prayed, and she committed the matter completely to God's will and was healed. The Lord heals because of the exercise of faith in His promises, whether it be through any true Christian's prayer, or those who have a special gift of healing (James 5:13–15).

If we are to have a strong faith so as to come boldly to the throne of grace (Hebrews 4:16), then we must do also, as we are taught in 1 John 3:22 (KJV), "And whatsoever we ask, we receive of him, because we keep His commandments and do those things that are pleasing in His sight."

There are some circumstances under which our Lord may not heal. It is appointed unto humans to die (Hebrews 9:27). Unbelief is a problem, and in Matthew 13:58 (KJV), we read, "And He did not many mighty works there because of unbelief." And there is unholy purpose: "Ye ask and receive not, because ye ask amiss, that ye may consume it upon your own lust" (James 4:3 KJV).

Some are not willing to do as the Bible says. "I beseech you therefore brethren, by the mercies of God, that ye present your bodies as a living sacrifice, holy, acceptable unto God, which is your reasonable service" (Romans 12:1 KJV). People who wreck their bodies through overwork, gluttony, the use of tobacco, and such should cooperate with God to allow Him to help them conquer such problems. This will help you to have faith for healing. Please look at 1 Corinthians 10:31 (KJV): "Whether therefore ye eat, or drink, or whatsoever ye do, do all to the glory of God."

Does the Lord Always Heal?

Several years ago, there was a minister of the church of God who was helping to take down a tent in which they had been conducting gospel meetings. While doing so, he had an accident.

Because of this accident, he was hurt to the extent that it left him an invalid for the rest of his life. I am sure he received healing to some extent from time to time, but he was never completely healed. Brother Naylor wrote several books. The title of one was *The Secret of a Singing Heart.* These books were a source of comfort and inspiration to many people.

Joni Earickson, who was paralyzed from her shoulders down in a swimming accident and has been that way for some fourteen years, is now in her thirties. She has this to say: "Why does God allow pain? We won't know all the answers until we get to Heaven."

It does seem that God permits some good, saved people to go through life with afflictions or sickness. I do not believe that we can always accuse them of not having faith or living close to God. Like Joni says, "We won't have all the answers until we get to Heaven."

Whether we have had a terrible accident that has crippled us for life, or we have a prolonged sickness, we can compare these situations in life with the apostle Paul's experience as given in 2 Corinthians 12:1–10—the thorn in the flesh that Paul speaks of in verses 7–9 verses and how he sought the Lord three times that it might be removed from him. The Lord said to him that His grace was sufficient for him.

William Barclay, in his commentary on 2 Corinthians, relates what different writers think the thorn in the flesh meant.

1. Spiritual temptations
2. Opposition and persecution
3. Carnal temptation
4. Paul's physical appearance
5. Epilepsy
6. Severe and prostrating headaches

7. Eye trouble
8. Malaria fever

Nobody seems to know just what the thorn in the flesh was. Barclay made this statement: "Paul prayed that the thorn might be taken from him, but God answered that prayer as he so often answers prayer. He did not take the thing away from him. He gave Paul strength to bear it. God does not spare us things. He makes us able to conquer them and to come through them."

From what I have read in recent years of the experiences of different Christians, I would say that the Lord does not always heal. Why, I do not know. Like the sons say, "We will understand it all by and by." Do not misunderstand. God does heal—I know He does—but not always in the way we think He should.

6

The Abrahamic Covenant and the Kingdom of God

Please read Genesis 17:1–7, Genesis 18:17–18, and Mark 1:14–15. God's covenant with Israel was a conditional covenant in its relationship with Israel as a nation, and in its relationship in a spiritual way in the New Testament. In the promise that God made to Abraham, we see that God's intention was to bring about the Jewish nation through Abraham's posterity. We also see in this covenant that God made with Abraham that, ultimately, all nations will be blessed.

The Jews were called God's chosen people (Deuteronomy 7:6–9). They were also called a peculiar people, meaning they were to be an exclusive people unto God (Deuteronomy 26:18). Note the condition: they were to keep all His commandments; see also Deuteronomy 30:15–20. They were not only to be a religious people with an exclusive style but also an exclusive people from a national standpoint. We see also that the promise that God made to Abraham contained two divisions of time: a time of national significance and a spiritual sense of time when it would take in all the people of the world who accepted Christ as their Savior. Some devout Jews were looking for Jesus to come into the world, and they recognized Him as the promised Messiah. Others did not. In all probability, more rejected Him than accepted Him.

In Luke 2:25–31, we read of one named Simeon, who was ready to receive Christ as the promised Messiah. Also, in the same chapter (verses 36–38), Anna was ready to receive Him. In the eighth chapter of John (verses 30–31), Christ told some who believed in Him that if they "continued in my word then are ye my disciples indeed." Of course, there were the apostles who accepted him, and also others on the day of Pentecost.

One of the saddest messages in the New Testament is the words found in the first chapter of the Gospel of John, verses 8–11. This speaks to us of the fact that many of Christ's own countrymen rejected Him. But in the twelfth verse we read, "But as many as received Him to them gave He the power to become the Sons of God, even to them that believe on His name."

The General Significance of the Covenant

In the promises that God made to Abraham, and his response to God in faith and obedience, the Bible tells us in Galatians 3:6 that his faith was accounted to him for righteousness. Abraham did not please God by doing the works of the law, because the law had not been given.

In Galatians 3:9 (KJV), we read, "So then they which be of faith are blessed with the faithful Abraham." In other words, Abraham was a forerunner or example of salvation by faith in the shed blood of Christ. This faith is the faith that is implanted in our hearts as a result of hearing the message of salvation as recorded in the gospel of the kingdom of God. The kingdom of God was established while Christ was here on earth; see Luke 17:21.

Duane Clarke

Why the Law Was Given

Adam Clarke, in his commentary on Galatians's third chapter, gives the following explanation.

> From the beginning God had proposed that salvation should be by faith and never expected that the soul of man should be justified by the works of the law; and only gave that law that the exceeding sinfulness of sin might appear, and that man be prepared to welcome the gospel, which proclaimed salvation to a lost world through the atoning passion and death of Christ.

Please read Galatians 3:24–26. The law was powerless to take away sin. That is, the animal blood offerings could not take away sin and give victory over sin; see Hebrews 10:1–10.

Now, considering the covenant that God made with Abraham, we see that there are two dispensations of time involved in the covenant that God made with Abraham: the dispensation of law and the dispensation of grace.

We are now living in the dispensation of grace. It began with the coming of Christ into the world and His dying on the cross of Calvary to purchase our salvation. It will last until the day our Lord returns to judge the world of sin and righteousness. The grace of God is extended to all the people of the world.

Titus 2:11 (NIV) reads, "The grace of God that bringeth salvation hath appeared to all me." Also read verses 12–14. Ephesians 2:8 (KJV) states, "For by grace are ye saved through faith; and that not of yourselves; It is the gift of God." And in the ninth verse it says, "Not of works, lest ay man should boast." In Romans 3:20–22, we see that by the deeds of the law, no person can be justified. The only way to be justified, and the only way to

108

be made righteous in God's sight, is by faith in Jesus Christ and obedience to His commandments. This plan of redemption in Christ is for all the peoples of the earth.

Notice particularly Galatians 3:28. In this present dispensation of grace, we see that Jew and Gentile are on the same level. All people need the Savior Jesus Christ, and after they become Christians, they are one in Christ. The only chosen people of God now are Christian people; see Titus 2:14 and 1 Peter 2:9. They are God's special people.

It seems that after the Galatian church was established, some Jews who came into their midst told them that along with their faith and trust in Christ for salvation, they would still have to keep the Mosaic law.

I would like for the reader to read Galatians 1:6–16 and Galatians 3:1–14. In these scriptures the apostle Paul deals with the problem. Note what Paul says in verse 13 of chapter 1. He speaks of his former life in the Jewish religion. When Paul became a Christian, he made a clean break with Judaism. He did allow an exception for a while, as in the case of Timothy (Acts 16:3; see also Romans 2:25–29). Here, he shows the difference between salvation through faith in Christ and the keeping of the rules and regulations of the law. However, he always had a strong love for his people, the Jews. He said, "My heart's desire and prayer to God for Israel is that they might be saved" (Romans 10:1 KJV).

All Christians love all the peoples of the world, but the chosen people of God are simply those who have accepted Christ and His gospel of salvation from sin through faith in the atonement that He made for our salvation on the cross of Calvary. Any system of salvation by ritualism and works will not save from sin. It took the blood sacrifice of Jesus to give victory over sin. We read in Colossians 3:11 (KJV) these words: "Where there is neither Greek nor Jew, circumcision nor uncircumcision, Barbarian, Synthian, bond nor free, but Christ is all and in all."

The Nature of the Kingdom of God

Jesus never spoke of His kingdom as being of this world or as being a material kingdom. In Luke 17:20–21 (KJV), we read, "The kingdom cometh not with observation; neither shall they say, lo here or lo there! For behold, the Kingdom of God is within you."

The church of God, the family of God, the kingdom of God, is not to be found in just one location on the map. The kingdom of God is in the heart of believers. In Revelation 3:20 (KJV), we read these words: "Behold I stand at the door and knock. If any man hear my voice, and open the door, I will come into him, and will sup with him, and he with me." Jesus is the door into His kingdom (John 10:9). Jesus is the only one who takes members into His church or kingdom (Acts 2:47).

Becoming a Christian, being born again, and being saved from sin is the requirement in becoming a member of His church or kingdom. The Bible tells us that in this dispensation of time, now is the time to be saved (2 Corinthians 6:1–2). This is God's acceptable time to be saved. There will be no other time to become a Christian other than in this present age. Both Jew and Gentile must either accept Him now or be lost forever. God puts no difference between Jew and Gentile in this gospel age (Romans 10:11–12). Some would tell us that in an age to come, the Jews will have a special time to accept Christ. To think of one group as being more chosen of God than another group would be racism. The Bible tells us that God is no respecter of persons (Acts 10:34–35). The Bible also says, "Whosoever will may come and take of the water of life freely" (Revelation 22:17 KJV). Humankind is free to accept God's offer or reject it.

Did you ever see the picture of Christ standing at the heart's door of humankind? There is no door knob on the outside. The door knob is on the inside. We must open our hearts' doors from the inside, of our own free will.

To say that God will give the Jews—or any other nation or person—a special time to accept Him is strictly unfounded by the scripture. God will never change humankind to make them willing to accept Him or His plan of redemption against their will.

After Christ returns and His children are caught up in the air to meet Him and go to live in the heaven that He is now preparing for those who love and serve Him, there will be no more time for others to prepare for His heaven (1 Thessalonians 4:17). The Bible teaches that now is the time to prepare for heaven by becoming born-again Christians. It's the time for both Jew and Gentile to prepare. Remember that there will be no other time. I cannot overemphasize this thought.

We Christians need to keep this in mind and work together to win the lost to Christ. Remember that Jesus declared that His kingdom was not of this world (John 18:36). It is in the heart of born-again Christians.

The gospel is for all people. In Matthew 11:28 we read, "Come unto Me all ye that Labor and are heavy laden, and I will give you rest." We read in Romans 3:9 that both Jews and Gentiles are under sin, and that both need a savior. It follows that Christ is the only means and that He paid the atonement for both!

We then understand that the judgment day will be for all people. Notice John 5:28–29 (KJV): "Marvel not at this, for the hour is coming, in which all the dead that are in the graves shall come forth; they that have done good into the resurrection of life; and they who have done evil into the resurrection of damnation." There is no way that this scripture could be interpreted to mean that there will be two resurrection days—one for the righteous and another for the wicked. Read 2 Thessalonians 1:7–10.

In Matthew 25:31–46, Jesus Himself describes what the judgment day will be like. Notice the minute description that He gave of the Christians being placed on His right side, the sinners on His left, and each group receiving something Those on the right receive the blessing of a heavenly reward, and those on the left get everlasting punishment. That describes perfectly what will take place on judgment day.

My idea of writing about the day of judgment in connection with the subject of the kingdom of God was for the purpose of showing that the kingdom of God is a present-day reality; see John 9:1 and Luke 16:16. You see, humans could not enter into something that did not exist if the kingdom was not a reality.

Second, now is the time to enjoy that experience; do not to wait for a kingdom yet to come. When our Lord returns for His bride, Christians will rise with Christ to go to heaven and enjoy the blessings of the kingdom forever and ever (1 Thessalonians 4:16–17).

On the judgment day, as well as after, it will be too late to enter the kingdom of God and become a part of it. We see in Revelation 10:1–2 and 6 that at the coming of Christ, an angel will appear with one foot on land and one foot on sea, declaring that time shall be no more.

7

Probation's End

I have already shown that God, in creating humankind, gave them the power of choice. They could decide to live by God's laws, morality, and righteousness, or they could reject them and live in sin against God.

During the lifetime of an individual, the Spirit of God deals with him or her and tries to woo and convince the person of the need to live by God's laws, and as in the present dispensation, to accept the gospel of Jesus Christ and live by its principles. This is called a probation period.

We see that according to Hebrews 7:25 and Hebrews 9:24, Christ is now seated at the right hand of God in heaven, making intercession for all humankind. Christ is our go-between man, and God is the Father. If we accept the offering of the shed blood of Christ on Calvary, God the Father will accept us and save us. If we accept Him now while we live, then the earlier in life we do so, the better off we are.

In 1 Corinthians 15, the apostle Paul has a lot to say about the second coming of Christ, the resurrection, and especially the righteous. I have already shown that on that day, the righteous and unrighteous will rise from their graves on the same day (John 5:28–29).

I would like for you to note the language of 1 Corinthians 15:24: "Then cometh the end." I understand that in the Greek language, *end* means "final, end." Also read verses 25–26. In Revelation 11:15, we read that Christ shall reign forever and ever.

So what does the scripture mean in 1 Corinthians 15:24, which says, "when He, Christ, shall have delivered up the kingdom to God"? This means He will deliver up the mediatorial aspects of His kingdom to the Father. The Holy Spirit will no longer convict the sinner; Christ will no longer intercede for the sinner. All opportunity for an individual to become a Christian will have passed.

All who want to go to heaven to enjoy the eternal happiness, the peace, and the beauty of heaven forever must be saved now. They must become Christians now, while they live in this world. All Jews and Gentiles must accept Christ, the promised Messiah. They must become Christians in the true sense of the word. Jews cannot hold on to Judaism and serve Christ at the same time.

The apostle Paul taught this truth in the Galatian epistle; please read John 8:21–24. Neither is there salvation in any other, for there is none other name under heaven given among men, whereby we must be saved.

Will There Be a Millennium?

For the most part, the Book of Revelation is written in symbols. I do not propose to go into a detailed study of Revelation 20. I would recommend that the reader obtain the book *The Symbols Speak* by Lillie McCutcheon; it can be obtained from Warner Press.

My desire is to treat the subject in the light of the plain statements of Christ in the Gospels of Matthew, Mark, Luke, and

John; in the Epistles of the apostles, Paul, Peter, and John; and throughout the book of Acts. There is nothing said by Christ or the apostles about a millennium. There is no place for a millennium, no time for a millennium. The texts millennialists use to try to prove the doctrine is Revelation 20:1–9. It is my understanding that the Revelation was written for the encouragement and comfort of God's children, in the early days of the history of the true church that Christ established while here on earth. It was during the period when God's people suffered severe persecution, and many became martyrs for the cause of Christ, His church, and the truth.

Romans 5:17 (KJV) says, "For, if by one man's offense death reigned by on; much more they which receive abundance of grace and of the gift of righteousness shall reign in life by one, Jesus Christ."

You see the severe persecution and death of some. Many Christians were able to live and endure it, but others lost their lives. Those who were able to live reigned with Christ in this world. The reign of some on earth was interrupted by death, but they still went right on reigning with Christ in paradise.

It is plain to see that we are not dealing with a literal thousand years here; it is symbolic. Notice the language of verse four. Sure enough, they reigned with Christ in paradise during that time of persecution, but they are still reigning with Christ in paradise now. You see, there is nothing said at all about a civil form of government of Christ on earth a thousand years.

No Time, No Need, No Place

I mentioned that there is no need, no time, and no place for a millennium. No need: I have mentioned that now is the day of salvation; see 2 Corinthians 6:2. There will be no other time but now to become a Christian, to get saved. In that sense, there's no future time in another age, and hence no need for a millennium. No place: In 2 Peter 3:10, we read that when Christ comes back, the earth will be burnt up. There will be no place to repent, and hence no millennium. There's one judgment day. No time: In 1 Corinthians 15:23–24, we see that the apostle Paul said that when Christ returns, that will be the end of time. Hence there is no millennium.

No Civil Government of Christ

To say that Christ will come back here and set up a civil government would be a humiliation for Christ. He is the King of kings and the Lord of lords (1 Timothy 6:15). He is now reigning and will continue to reign, but not on earth now or ever. He doesn't need to. But He is reigning in the hearts of believers.

The battle of Armageddon is not a literal battle. It was and still is the forces of right against the forces of evil. Notice in Matthew 26:51–52 that we find Christ telling Peter to put his sword away when he was about to fight for Christ at the time preceding His trial before Pilate. Christ's kingdom was not of this world. He said that if it were, His servants would fight for Him.

Ephesians 6:12 speaks to us very clearly as to what the nature of this warfare is to a Christian. It is against the powers of spiritual darkness. This is not to say that God would never interfere with some civil government on earth; see 1 Chronicles 29:12 and Psalm 83:8. That is as long as time lasts. Then comes the final judgment.

The Final Sign of the Judgment Day

We read in Acts 1:9–11 of our Lord's return to heaven after His ministry on earth. While His apostles watched Him ascend unto heaven, two angels stood near them and said to the apostles that Christ would come back in like manner: "As ye have seen

Him go into Heaven, Christ will suddenly appear" (Matthew 24:27).

The Bible does not say that Christ will ever touch His feet on earth again. Notice how 1 Thessalonians 4:14–17 reads. I will paraphrase parts of these verses. Christ will descend from heaven with a shout, with a strong trumpet sound. The dead in Christ will rise first. Live saints on earth will be caught up in the air to meet the Lord and the resurrected saints of the past, and they'll go to be forever with the Lord. Please read Matthew 25:31–46 to see what the procedure will be in giving out the rewards of the righteous, who have been faithful in the Christian life while here on earth. Then judgment will be pronounced on all the wicked. This does not allow for two judgment days. All these things will take place on the last day of planet earth. All will take place when our Lord returns the second time. Remember to rightly divide God's Word.

Here are some further thoughts on Christ's coming. We read that when Christ comes, every eye shall see Him. They also which pierced Him. It will be a day of wailing for some, a day of extreme happiness for the saved. See Revelation 1:7 and John 14:1–3.

There will be no end of the blessings in heaven for the born-again Christians. There will be no end of torment in hell for the wicked and those who know not Christ as Savior and Lord of their lives. Our Lord will not come back in weakness; He will come in power and great glory (Luke 21:27).

We do not need to speculate as to when He is coming, having our sins already washed in the blood of the Lamb, having been faithful to our calling in Christ Jesus. We are warned in the scripture to watch for His coming (Matthew 24:42; Mark 13:33).

The watchword is to be faithful unto death or until Christ comes. See Matthew 24:45–46 and 1 Peter 5:8–9; also read 2 Peter 2:9. We see here that God will keep us faithful if we trust and obey Him. The wicked will be judged and condemned on judgment day.

What glorious words of the Master to hear Him say, "Come, ye blessed of my Father, inherit the kingdom prepared for you from the foundation of the world." We can be members of the kingdom of God now and go to heaven, inheriting the eternal kingdom.

Come, ye blessed Jew, Greek, and people of every nation. What a glorious sight to behold! Heaven must be a wonderful place!

Like the song by Jim Hill says,

> There is coming a day when no heartaches shall come,
>
> No more clouds in the sky, no more tears to dim the eye;
>
> All is peace for evermore on that happy golden shore.
>
> What a day that will be, when My Jesus I shall see,
>
> And I look upon His face, the one who saved me by his grace.
>
> When He takes me by the hand, and leads me through the Promised land, What a day, glorious day, that will be.

I want to dedicate this book to my family and to my son Noel, who died of cancer at fifty years old. What a nice tribute they gave my son in Moundsville, West Virginia.

In Loving Memory of Noel E. Clarke

July 30, 1967–November 9, 2017

Many have no idea why we do the job. It's not for everyone, and that has become very apparent. This job is about your team and the people you serve. It should consume you to the point that you strive to make order out of chaos every time the rig rolls out the door. This isn't a game. It's real life. Our friends and neighbors depend on us in their darkest hours. My once-white helmet is now black for a reason. My body aches from years of pounding. My heart hurts from the sadness I have seen. However, it's what needs to be done that keeps me going. It runs through my blood to the point that it is burnt into my soul. It's all that I know, and the sad part is it has cost me so much. In the end, I hope that I made a difference.

Noel Clarke

Fire Chief

Noel Clarke Obituary

Noel E. "Noelski" "Stretch" Clarke, 50, of Moundsville, West Virginia, died Thursday, November 9, 2017, in Wheeling Hospital.

He was born July 30, 1967, in Glen Dale, West Virginia, the son of Russell Duane (Linda) Clarke and the late Sheri Ramsden Clarke.

He served as fire chief for the Moundsville Fire Department since 2002, having joined the department on July 31, 1997.

Noel was a Christian by faith, a big sports fan, an avid hunter, and a fisherman, and he coached baseball for many years.

He enjoyed spending time with his friends at Fish Creek, whether while riding ATVs, sitting by the campfire, or, more importantly, laughing with friends.

It gave Noel great pleasure and satisfaction knowing that he helped to mold the new generation of fire fighters that have also chosen to sacrifice their time for such a great cause. Noel truly made a difference.

In addition to his father and stepmother, survivors include a son, Brady Clarke of Moundsville; a sister, Sonya (Matt) Kennedy of Gahanna, Ohio; two brothers, Duane (Bevy) Clarke of King George, Virginia, and Steve (Kelly) Clarke of Jacksonville, North Carolina; and several aunts, uncles, nieces and nephews.

Family will receive friends on Sunday and Monday from 2–4 and 6–8 p.m. at Grisell Funeral Home and Crematory, 500 Jefferson Avenue, Moundsville, where funeral services will be held Tuesday at 1 p.m. with Pastor Mike Eskridge officiating.

The Moundsville Fire Department will be conducting full firefighter honors.

Fire Chief Clarke Dies at 50

It was a somber Friday at the Moundsville Fire Department as firefighters mourned the loss of Fire Chief Noel Clarke, who died Thursday at age 50 after a long battle with cancer.

Clarke had been a member of the fire department since 1997, becoming chief in 2002. Assistant Fire Chief Ron Walker stood talking with his coworkers outside the building Friday morning, recalling Clarke's dedication to his community and to his job.

"He was a leader, he was an instructor, and he was a teacher," Walker said. "He really helped a lot of people over the years, and he always put the community and the people first."

Despite his illness, Walker said, Clarke remained on the job almost to the very end, taking care of business as usual.

Moundsville police Sergeant Don DeWitt recalled Clarke's positive attitude, which never wavered over the course of his career. DeWitt noted Clarke's dedication to his job even while he was fighting for his life.

"I worked with him for twenty years, and he always had a smile on his face," DeWitt said. "Even after being diagnosed, he still chose to serve the community. If that doesn't say enough about him, I don't know what will. He was a good man and a huge loss to Moundsville."

Vice Mayor David Wood said he admired Clarke's openness and willingness to speak his mind.

"He was straightforward. You never had to wonder what he was thinking—he'd tell you," Wood said. "In my opinion, his personality was (that) he could make you laugh, he could be very serious, and he could make you think… When I worked in the school system and as a councilperson, Noel would do anything to help with the children and students. He was a quality person."

Clarke is survived by his son, Brady, as well as his father, several siblings, and other relatives.

Walker said a firefighter's service is planned for Clarke at his funeral, which is scheduled for 1 p.m. Tuesday at Grisell Funeral Home in Moundsville.

Printed in the United States
By Bookmasters